BUILDING WEALTH

Navigating The Pathway to Financial

Freedom

JACK STEWART

Copyright

Disclaimer

The information provided in this book, "Building Wealth: Navigating The Pathway to Financial Freedom," is intended for general informational purposes only. The author and publisher are not engaged in providing financial, legal, or professional advice. Readers are encouraged to seek the counsel of qualified professionals for personalized financial guidance. The author and publisher make no representations or warranties regarding the accuracy or completeness of the information presented herein and shall not be liable for any errors or omissions. The reader assumes sole responsibility for any financial decisions or actions taken based on the information in this book.

Table of content

Introduction

In a world where financial stability is more crucial than ever, the pursuit of true freedom—financial freedom—has become a driving force for individuals seeking to carve out their destinies on their terms. Welcome to "Building Wealth: Navigating the Pathway to Financial Freedom." This journey you're about to embark upon is more than just a roadmap; it's a transformative experience that will empower you to seize control of your financial future.

Imagine a life where your decisions are not dictated by the limitations of your bank account, where opportunities aren't missed due to financial constraints, and where you have the power to shape your aspirations into reality. This is the promise of financial freedom—an open horizon of possibilities that allows you to live life on your own terms, unshackled by the worries of paycheck-to-paycheck existence.

In the pages that follow, we will navigate the intricate landscape of wealth building, arming you with the knowledge, strategies, and mindset needed to journey towards lasting financial freedom. We'll explore the fundamental principles of personal finance, the art of intelligent investing, the creation of diversified income streams, and the wisdom of protecting your hard-earned assets. This book is not a quick-fix scheme or a promise of instant riches; rather, it's a comprehensive guide that equips you with the tools to architect a solid financial foundation.

But building wealth is more than just dollars and cents; it's about mindset and intention. It's about fostering a mindset that embraces abundance, cultivates discipline, and embraces the long-term perspective. Through anecdotes of both triumphs and trials, you'll gain insights into the mental fortitude required to weather storms and celebrate victories along this journey.

You'll explore the world of entrepreneurship, witnessing the transformation of ideas into thriving businesses that not only fuel your passions but also generate income. You'll delve into the realm of investments, discovering how calculated risks can yield exponential rewards over time. And you'll uncover the secrets of preserving and passing on your wealth, ensuring that your legacy endures for generations.

No journey is without challenges, and the path to financial freedom is no exception. But as you face setbacks and uncertainties, remember that each obstacle is an opportunity to learn, adapt, and grow. This book will be your guide, your confidant, and your source of inspiration as you navigate the twists and turns of your personal financial landscape.

So, whether you're starting from scratch, looking to accelerate your progress, or aiming to secure your legacy, "Building

Wealth: Navigating the Pathway to Financial Freedom" is your companion on this remarkable voyage. The knowledge you gain and the actions you take will reshape not only your financial future but also the way you view the world. The time to embark on this journey is now—because your financial freedom is waiting to be claimed.

Understanding the Importance of Financial Freedom

Financial freedom, like a hidden treasure buried within the vast landscape of life, holds the key to unlocking doors you never knew existed. It's not just about having an abundance of money; it's about the liberation that comes from having control over your financial choices, enabling you to live a life aligned with your deepest aspirations.

Imagine waking up each morning with the knowledge that you're not bound by the constraints of bills, debts, and financial obligations. Consider the peace of mind that comes from knowing you have the resources to weather unexpected storms, pursue your passions, and support your loved ones. This is the essence of financial freedom—an empowerment that transcends mere dollars and cents.

At its core, financial freedom is the bridge between dreams and reality. It allows you to bridge the gap between wanting to travel the world and actually buying that plane ticket. It transforms your desire to provide the best education for your children from a wish into a tangible goal. It turns the idea of retiring comfortably into a well-orchestrated plan.

In a world where financial uncertainty is a constant companion, attaining financial freedom becomes an act of self-care. It's a declaration that you value your own well-being and that of those you care for. It's about seizing the reins of your life and steering it in the direction of abundance and security.

However, understanding the importance of financial freedom requires recognizing that it's not a destination, but a journey—a dynamic process that involves intention, knowledge, and action. It's a journey that's as much about the mind as it is about money. Developing a mindset that aligns with financial freedom means cultivating habits of discipline, budgeting, and long-term thinking.

Financial freedom also empowers you to give back to your community, support causes you're passionate about, and make a positive impact on the world. When you're not constantly struggling to make ends meet, you can focus on contributing to the greater good in meaningful ways.

Moreover, financial freedom provides a safety net—an assurance that even in times of economic upheaval, you have the foundation to stand firm. It's about breaking free from the paycheck-to-paycheck cycle and stepping into a realm of possibilities where your decisions aren't dictated solely by monetary concerns.

In the chapters that follow, you'll explore the multifaceted aspects of building wealth and achieving financial freedom. You'll discover strategies to manage your money wisely, grow your income streams, invest with purpose, and safeguard your assets.

But remember, the pursuit of financial freedom is not about amassing wealth for its own sake; it's about designing a life that reflects your values, passions, and aspirations.

As you embark on this journey, keep in mind that each step you take, each lesson you learn, and each choice you make is a stride toward greater autonomy and self-determination. The importance of financial freedom isn't just about reaching a distant goal; it's about embracing a new way of life—an empowered life where you are the author of your financial story.

Setting the Stage for Wealth Building

Imagine wealth building as constructing a grand edifice—a majestic structure that stands the test of time. Just as a magnificent building starts with a well-designed blueprint and a solid foundation, your journey toward wealth begins with thoughtful planning and a strong financial base.

Before you lay the first brick of your wealth-building endeavor, it's essential to set the stage for success. This involves laying the groundwork, clarifying your intentions, and establishing a clear path forward.

1. **Define Your "Why"**

- Begin by asking yourself: Why do you seek wealth? Is it to provide a secure future for your family? To have the freedom to pursue your passions? To make a difference in the lives of others? Defining your "why" will serve as your compass, guiding your decisions and actions as you navigate the complexities of wealth building.

2. Assess Your Current Financial Situation

- Take a candid look at your current financial landscape. Calculate your assets, liabilities, income, and expenses. This snapshot will serve as a starting point—a reference against which you can measure your progress. It's crucial to have a clear understanding of where you stand before you begin charting your course.

3. Set Clear and Achievable Goals

- Like milestones on a journey, goals provide direction and motivation. Outline short-term and long-term goals that reflect your aspirations. Make them specific, measurable, achievable, relevant, and time-bound (SMART). Whether it's buying a home, funding your children's education, or retiring comfortably, well-defined goals will give your wealth-building journey purpose and structure.

4. Create a Budget and Manage Debt

- A budget is your financial compass, ensuring you stay on track toward your goals. Allocate your income to essential expenses, savings, investments, and discretionary spending. Strive to live below your means to free up resources for wealth accumulation. Additionally, address any existing debt strategically to minimize its impact on your financial journey.

5. Build an Emergency Fund

- Life is full of surprises, and having an emergency fund is like having a safety net to catch you when unexpected challenges arise. Aim to save three to six months' worth of living expenses in a separate, easily accessible account. This fund will provide peace of mind and prevent financial setbacks from derailing your progress.

6. Invest in Your Financial Education

- Knowledge is the cornerstone of wealth building. Dedicate time to educate yourself about personal finance, investment strategies, and money management. Attend seminars, read books, and leverage online resources to enhance your financial literacy. A well-informed approach will empower you to make informed decisions and navigate the complexities of the financial world.

7. Cultivate Discipline and Patience

- Wealth building is a marathon, not a sprint. It requires discipline to stick to your budget, patience to weather market fluctuations, and the resolve to stay committed even when progress seems slow. Remember that small, consistent actions compound over time to create substantial results.

Setting the stage for wealth building is not a one-time event but an ongoing process. It involves aligning your financial choices with your values and aspirations, and it lays the groundwork for the chapters that lie ahead. As you embark on this journey, keep your "why" in focus and embrace the journey itself—because the foundation you build today will support the grand structure of your financial future.

The Foundation: Financial Mindset and Goals

Just as a sturdy foundation is essential for a towering skyscraper, a solid financial mindset and clear goals are the bedrock of your wealth-building journey. Your mindset shapes your actions, and your goals provide the direction and purpose needed to navigate the path ahead. In this chapter, we delve into the crucial role that your mindset and goals play in building and sustaining wealth.

Cultivating a Wealth-Building Mindset

Your mindset is the lens through which you perceive the world and make decisions. Cultivating a wealth-building mindset is akin to refining your mental blueprint for success. Here are key principles to adopt:

1. Abundance Mentality: Embrace the belief that opportunities are abundant and success is achievable. Replace thoughts of scarcity with thoughts of abundance, recognizing that the world is full of possibilities waiting to be seized.

2. Long-Term Perspective: Shift your focus from immediate gratification to long-term gain. Understand that true wealth building is a patient process that involves delayed gratification and consistent effort over time.

3. Continuous Learning: Approach financial education as an ongoing journey. Stay curious and open to learning about new

investment strategies, money management techniques, and economic trends.

4. Resilience: Understand that setbacks are part of the journey. Develop the resilience to overcome challenges, adapt to changing circumstances, and learn from failures.

5. Positive Relationship with Money: Release any negative emotions or associations you might have with money. View money as a tool for achieving your goals and improving your quality of life.

Setting Clear and Achievable Financial Goals

Goals are the guiding stars that keep you on course as you navigate the sea of financial decisions. They give you purpose, motivate your actions, and measure your progress. Here's how to set effective financial goals:

1. Specificity: Define your goals with precision. Instead of vague goals like "be rich," specify how much wealth you aim to accumulate, by when, and for what purpose.

2. Measurability: Ensure that your goals are quantifiable. This allows you to track your progress objectively and celebrate milestones along the way.

3. Achievability: While aiming high is admirable, set goals that are realistic and attainable based on your current resources, skills, and circumstances.

4. Relevance: Your goals should align with your values and aspirations. Make sure they resonate with your core beliefs and reflect what truly matters to you.

5. Time-Bound: Set deadlines for your goals. A timeframe creates a sense of urgency and prevents procrastination.

6. Breakdown into Milestones: Break down larger goals into smaller, achievable milestones. This prevents overwhelm and provides a clear roadmap for progression.

By nurturing a mindset of abundance, resilience, and continuous learning, and by setting well-defined, meaningful goals, you lay a strong foundation for your journey to financial freedom. Your mindset will be the engine that propels you forward, and your goals will be the compass that keeps you on track. As you proceed, remember that your mindset and goals will evolve and adapt—just as a building's foundation supports growth and expansion.

Cultivating a Wealth-Building Mindset

In the realm of wealth-building, your mind is the fertile soil from which your financial success will grow. Just as a gardener tends to their plants, you must nurture and cultivate a mindset that aligns with your aspirations. A wealth-building mindset isn't merely about money; it's about adopting attitudes and beliefs that empower you to make wise decisions, overcome challenges, and seize opportunities. Here's how to cultivate this invaluable mindset:

1. Embrace Abundance:
Shift your perspective from scarcity to abundance. Recognize that the world is abundant with opportunities, ideas, and

resources. An abundance mindset allows you to see possibilities where others might see limitations, opening doors to innovative ventures and creative solutions.

2. Think Long-Term:
Wealth-building is a marathon, not a sprint. Embrace the power of delayed gratification and understand that small, consistent efforts over time lead to substantial results. Think beyond immediate gains and focus on the enduring benefits of your actions.

3. Welcome Learning and Growth:
Treat every experience as a lesson. Embrace a thirst for knowledge about personal finance, investments, and economic trends. Continuously seek to expand your

understanding, and be open to adapting your strategies based on new information.

4. Develop Resilience:

Setbacks are part of any journey. Cultivate resilience by viewing challenges as opportunities for growth. Learn from your failures, adjust your course, and persevere. A resilient mindset equips you to weather storms and emerge stronger on the other side.

5. Transform Risk into Opportunity:

Risk is an inherent aspect of wealth-building. Rather than avoiding risk, learn to manage and leverage it. Understand that calculated risks can lead to substantial rewards. A wealth-building mindset reframes risk as a chance to grow and innovate.

6. Practice Gratitude:
Gratitude is a powerful tool that shifts your focus from what you lack to what you have. By appreciating your current resources, you create a positive atmosphere that fosters abundance and attracts further opportunities.

7. Associate with Like-Minded Individuals:
Surround yourself with people who share your values and aspirations. Engage in conversations that uplift and inspire, and learn from those who have successfully walked the path you're embarking on.

8. Visualize Success:

Create a vivid mental image of your financial success. Visualization helps align your subconscious mind with your goals, making you more attuned to opportunities that bring you closer to realizing your vision.

9. Cultivate Patience:
Wealth-building takes time, and patience is your ally. Avoid the allure of get-rich-quick schemes and focus on steady progress. Patience allows you to make well-considered decisions that stand the test of time.

10. Practice Generosity:
As paradoxical as it may seem, practicing generosity is a key aspect of a wealth-building mindset. Contributing to others and giving back not only aligns with

abundance but also creates a positive ripple effect that can enhance your overall success.

Cultivating a wealth-building mindset is a continuous journey of self-discovery and growth. It's about rewiring your thoughts, beliefs, and habits to align with the financial future you envision. Remember, just as a garden needs consistent care and attention, your mindset requires nurturing and reinforcement. With each step you take, you're not just building wealth; you're crafting a mindset that will serve as the cornerstone of your financial success.

Setting Clear and Achievable Financial Goals

Goals are the compass that guides you through the labyrinth of wealth-building, ensuring you stay on track and make purposeful decisions. Setting clear and achievable financial goals is like plotting coordinates on a map—it helps you navigate the path to your desired destination with clarity and determination. Here's how to set goals that propel you toward financial success:

1. Be Specific:
Vague goals yield vague results. Define your goals with precision. Instead of saying, "I want to be wealthy," specify the amount you

aim to accumulate, such as "I want to have $1 million in savings and investments."

2. Make Them Measurable:
A measurable goal is one you can track and quantify. Assign numbers and metrics to your goals. This allows you to gauge progress objectively and celebrate milestones along the way.

3. Ensure Achievability:
While dreaming big is important, set goals that are realistically attainable based on your current resources, skills, and circumstances. Setting unattainable goals can lead to frustration and discouragement.

4. Align with Your Values:

Your goals should reflect your values, priorities, and aspirations. Make sure they resonate deeply with you. When your goals align with what matters most, you'll be more motivated to pursue them with passion.

5. Set Time-Bound Deadlines:
Without a timeframe, goals can become distant aspirations. Set specific deadlines for achieving your goals. A timeframe adds a sense of urgency and prevents procrastination.

6. Break Down into Smaller Steps:
Large goals can be overwhelming. Break them down into smaller, manageable steps. Each step becomes an achievable milestone that propels you forward and boosts your confidence.

7. Create Short-Term and Long-Term Goals:
Distinguish between short-term and long-term goals. Short-term goals might include building an emergency fund or paying off credit card debt. Long-term goals could involve purchasing a home or retiring comfortably.

8. Write Them Down:
Putting your goals in writing makes them tangible and reinforces your commitment. Keep your goals in a visible place to serve as a constant reminder of what you're working toward.

9. Review and Adjust Regularly:
Your financial journey is dynamic. Regularly review and adjust your goals as

circumstances change. Life events, economic shifts, and personal growth might warrant updates to your goals.

10. Stay Flexible and Open-Minded:
While goals provide direction, be open to opportunities and changes along the way. Sometimes unexpected paths lead to the most rewarding outcomes. Adaptability is a valuable trait on your wealth-building journey.

Setting clear and achievable financial goals empowers you to make intentional decisions that align with your vision of success. Your goals act as guideposts, helping you stay focused and motivated even in the face of challenges. Remember that your goals are not fixed; they can evolve and adapt as you grow. Each goal you achieve is a step closer to the life you envision—one that's characterized by financial security, freedom, and the realization of your dreams.

Mastering Personal Finance

At the heart of successful wealth-building lies the mastery of personal finance. Just as a craftsman hones their skills, you too must refine your financial acumen to build a strong foundation for your journey. Mastering personal finance empowers you to take control of your money, make informed decisions, and lay the groundwork for a prosperous future. Here's how to navigate this essential aspect of wealth-building:

1. Craft a Budget:
A budget is your financial roadmap. Track your income and categorize your expenses, including essentials, discretionary spending, and savings. Creating a budget ensures that

your money is allocated purposefully and helps you live within your means.

2. Prioritize Savings:

Pay yourself first by prioritizing savings. Establish an emergency fund to cover unforeseen expenses, and set up regular contributions to retirement and investment accounts. Saving early and consistently takes advantage of the power of compounding.

3. Reduce Debt Wisely:

Manage and reduce debt strategically. Prioritize high-interest debts and create a repayment plan. Avoid accumulating unnecessary debt and consider refinancing options to lower interest rates.

4. Live Below Your Means:

Resist the temptation to spend every dollar you earn. Living below your means frees up resources for saving and investing, accelerating your journey toward financial freedom.

5. Build an Investment Strategy:

Investing is the engine of wealth growth. Educate yourself about different investment vehicles, such as stocks, bonds, real estate, and mutual funds. Craft an investment strategy that aligns with your risk tolerance and financial goals.

6. Diversify Your Portfolio:

Spread your investments across different asset classes to reduce risk. Diversification helps safeguard your wealth against the potential downfall of a single investment.

7. Be Tax-Efficient:

Understand how taxes impact your earnings and investments. Explore tax-advantaged accounts, deductions, and strategies that minimize your tax liability and maximize your wealth.

8. Continuous Learning:

Stay updated with financial news and trends. Attend workshops, read books, and follow reputable financial sources. The more informed you are, the better equipped you'll be to make sound financial decisions.

9. Avoid Impulse Spending:

Practice mindful spending by distinguishing between needs and wants. Avoid impulsive purchases and make spending decisions based on your financial goals.

10. Reevaluate Regularly:
Life changes, and so should your financial plan. Regularly review your budget, investments, and goals. Adjust your plan as needed to accommodate new circumstances.

11. Seek Professional Guidance:
Consider consulting a financial advisor or planner. Their expertise can help you create a comprehensive financial strategy tailored to your unique goals and circumstances.

Mastering personal finance is an ongoing journey that requires discipline, education, and a willingness to adapt. By taking control of your money, you gain the power to shape your financial destiny. As you progress on this path, you'll not only build wealth but also develop a sense of financial empowerment that will impact every facet of your life.

Budgeting Strategies for Effective Money Management

A well-crafted budget serves as your financial compass, guiding you toward your wealth-building goals with purpose and control. Budgeting isn't about restricting your lifestyle; it's about making intentional choices that align with your priorities. Here are effective budgeting strategies to help you manage your money wisely:

**1. Track Your Income and Expenses:
Begin by documenting your sources of income and all your expenses. Categorize your expenses into fixed (e.g., rent, mortgage) and variable (e.g., entertainment, dining out) categories.

**2. Create a Zero-Based Budget:

In this approach, every dollar you earn is allocated to a specific category, leaving no unassigned funds. This ensures that every aspect of your finances is accounted for, from savings to bills to discretionary spending.

**3. Use the 50/30/20 Rule:

Allocate 50% of your income to needs (essential expenses like housing and utilities), 30% to wants (non-essential expenses like entertainment and dining out), and 20% to savings and debt repayment.

**4. Envelope Budgeting:

Assign cash to different envelopes for specific spending categories. When an envelope is empty, you've reached your spending limit for that category. This method encourages mindful spending.

**5. Digital Budgeting Tools:
Numerous apps and online tools help you create, track, and manage your budget. They often sync with your bank accounts, making it easier to monitor transactions and keep your budget up-to-date.

**6. Automate Savings and Bills:
Set up automatic transfers to your savings and investment accounts right after you receive your paycheck. Also, automate bill payments to avoid late fees and ensure you're staying within your budget.

**7. Prioritize Debt Repayment:

If you have outstanding debts, allocate a portion of your budget to repay them systematically. Focus on high-interest debts first while making minimum payments on others.

**8. Review and Adjust Regularly:
Your financial situation and goals change over time. Regularly review your budget to make sure it's still aligned with your priorities. Adjust as needed to accommodate new circumstances.

**9. Emergency Fund Allocation:
Include contributions to your emergency fund in your budget. Having a cushion for unexpected expenses helps you avoid derailing your budget when unforeseen situations arise.

**10. Practice Frugality Mindfully:

Trimming unnecessary expenses is commendable, but ensure it's done mindfully. Focus on areas that align with your values, and allocate the savings to goals that matter to you.

**11. Set Goals within Your Budget:

Allocate specific funds to short-term and long-term goals within your budget. This ensures you're consistently progressing toward your financial aspirations.

Budgeting isn't about rigidity; it's about taking control and directing your financial resources toward what truly matters to you. By embracing these budgeting strategies, you'll gain clarity, reduce financial stress, and forge a path toward achieving your wealth-building goals. Remember, your budget is a tool that empowers you to make intentional choices that align with your dreams and aspirations.

Saving and Investing: Building Blocks of Wealth

Saving and investing are the twin pillars upon which the edifice of wealth is constructed. They form the cornerstone of your financial journey, providing the means to grow your resources and achieve your goals. While often used interchangeably, saving and investing are distinct strategies that work in tandem to fortify your financial foundation.

Saving: The Foundation of Financial Security

Saving is the act of setting aside a portion of your income for future use. It creates a safety net that shields you from unexpected expenses and provides the liquidity needed for short-term goals. Here's how saving lays the groundwork for your financial security:

- Emergency Fund: An emergency fund is your financial buffer against unforeseen events like medical emergencies or job loss. Aim to save three to six months' worth of living expenses in an easily accessible account.
- Short-Term Goals: Saving helps you achieve short-term objectives like buying a car, taking a vacation, or making a down payment on a house. Having funds readily available ensures you can seize opportunities as they arise.
- Debt Management: Savings can be used to pay off high-interest debts,

reducing financial stress and saving money on interest payments.

Investing: The Engine of Wealth Growth

Investing involves putting your money to work in vehicles that have the potential to generate returns over time. Unlike saving, which preserves your principal, investing aims to grow your wealth. Here's how investing propels your journey to financial independence:

- Compound Interest: Investments have the power of compounding on their side. Over time, your earnings generate more earnings, accelerating the growth of your wealth.
- Beat Inflation: Inflation erodes the purchasing power of your money. By

investing, you aim to achieve returns that outpace inflation, ensuring your money retains its value.

- Long-Term Goals: Investments are instrumental in achieving long-term goals like retirement planning, funding education, or building generational wealth.
- Diversification: Through investments, you can diversify your portfolio across different asset classes, reducing risk and enhancing the potential for stable returns.

Harmonizing Saving and Investing: A Comprehensive Approach

While saving provides security and liquidity, investing offers the potential for growth and long-term financial success. A balanced approach involves:

- Emergency Fund: Prioritize building a solid emergency fund before making substantial investments. This ensures you're financially prepared for unexpected challenges.
- Investment Goals: Set clear investment goals, such as retirement, education, or wealth accumulation. Tailor your investment strategy to align with these objectives.
- Risk Tolerance: Assess your risk tolerance and choose investments that match your comfort level. Remember that risk and return are often correlated—the greater the potential return, the higher the risk.
- Diversification: Spread your investments across different asset

classes to minimize risk. This can include stocks, bonds, real estate, and other investment vehicles.

- Consistency: Regularly contribute to your investments to take advantage of compounding. Even small, consistent contributions can have a significant impact over time.

Saving and investing are intertwined disciplines that propel you toward financial freedom. Saving provides the stability and resources you need for short-term goals and emergencies, while investing has the potential to generate significant wealth over the long term. By understanding and harmonizing these two building blocks, you're poised to create a robust financial future that aligns with your aspirations.

Remember, it's not just about how much you earn, but how effectively you save and invest that sets the course for your journey to prosperity.

Exploring Different Income Streams

Diversifying your sources of income is like planting seeds in various fields—you're not reliant on a single harvest, and your financial landscape becomes more resilient. Exploring different income streams empowers you to create stability, enhance your earning potential, and accelerate your journey toward financial freedom. Here's how to uncover and cultivate various income streams:

1. Earned Income: Your Primary Source
Earned income is the money you receive in exchange for your time and skills. It's typically your primary source of income and comes from employment or

self-employment. To maximize earned income:

- Invest in education and skill development to increase your earning potential.
- Explore opportunities for career advancement, promotions, or salary negotiations.
- Consider freelancing, consulting, or side gigs to supplement your primary income.

2. Passive Income: Earning While You Sleep Passive income flows in even when you're not actively working. It requires upfront effort but can generate continuous returns. Common passive income sources include:

- Rental Income: Invest in real estate properties and generate rental income from tenants.
- Dividend Stocks: Invest in stocks that pay dividends, providing a share of the company's profits to shareholders.
- Royalties: If you have creative works like books, music, or art, you can earn royalties whenever they're used or sold.

3. Portfolio Income: Capital Appreciation

Portfolio income comes from the appreciation of your investments. As the value of your investments increases, you can sell them for a profit. Common sources of portfolio income include:

- Stocks and Bonds: Buy assets that have the potential to appreciate over time, then sell them at a higher value.
- Real Estate: Invest in properties with the intention of selling them at a profit when their value increases.

4. Residual Income: Work Once, Earn Repeatedly

Residual income is earned from work done in the past that continues to generate income. This can come from:

- Online Businesses: Create digital products, courses, or content that people can purchase, generating income over time.
- Network Marketing: Build a network of customers and distributors to earn ongoing commissions from sales.

5. Business Income: Entrepreneurship

Starting a business can be a potent income source. It requires significant effort and risk upfront but can lead to substantial rewards:

- Traditional Businesses: Start a business in an area you're passionate about, solving a problem or meeting a need in the market.
- Online Businesses: E-commerce, digital services, and other online ventures offer global reach and scalability.

6. Investment Income: Financial Instruments

Investment income is generated from interest, dividends, and capital gains on financial instruments like bonds, stocks, and mutual funds. Here's how to optimize investment income:

- Interest-Bearing Accounts: Invest in high-yield savings accounts, certificates of deposit (CDs), or bonds to earn interest.
- Dividend Stocks: Select dividend-paying stocks that provide a regular stream of income.

7. Rental Income: Real Estate Ventures

Rental income is earned from leasing out properties you own. Real estate can be a stable income source:

- Residential Properties: Rent out apartments, houses, or condominiums to tenants.
- Commercial Properties: Lease office or retail spaces to businesses.

8. Side Hustles and Freelancing: Flexibility and Autonomy

Side hustles and freelancing offer flexibility and autonomy, allowing you to earn extra income outside of your primary job:

- Freelancing: Offer services like writing, design, programming, or consulting on a freelance basis.
- Gig Economy: Join platforms that connect you with clients seeking short-term services.

9. Intellectual Property: Creativity as an Asset

If you possess creative talents, your intellectual property can become a source of income:

- Books and E-books: Write and publish books or e-books on various platforms.
- Art and Crafts: Sell your artwork, crafts, or digital designs online.

10. Real Estate Crowdfunding: Passive Real Estate Investment

Real estate crowdfunding platforms allow you to invest in real estate projects collectively with other investors. It provides access to real estate investment without the need to own and manage properties directly.

11. Peer-to-Peer Lending: Lending as an Investment

Through peer-to-peer lending platforms, you can lend money to individuals or small businesses in exchange for interest payments, diversifying your investment portfolio.

12. Teaching and Coaching: Share Your Expertise

If you have specialized knowledge or skills, you can monetize them through teaching, coaching, or consulting:

- Online Courses: Create and sell online courses on platforms like Udemy or Teachable.
- Personal Coaching: Offer one-on-one coaching in areas like fitness, business, or personal development.

13. Affiliate Marketing: Promote Products for Commission

Affiliate marketing involves promoting products or services and earning a commission for every sale made through your referral:

- Blogging and Content Creation: Incorporate affiliate links into your content to earn commissions on recommended products.
- Social Media: Promote products on platforms like Instagram, YouTube, or TikTok, earning commissions for sales generated through your links.

14. Licensing Your Ideas: Monetize Your Innovations

If you have inventive ideas, you can license them to companies that can turn them into products:

- Patents: If you have a patent-worthy invention, you can license it to companies for manufacturing and distribution.
- Product Designs: Sell your product designs to manufacturers or retailers.

15. Rental Platforms: Sharing Economy

Use platforms like Airbnb or Turo to rent out your property or assets, such as your home, a spare room, or your car, to earn extra income.

16. Content Creation: Digital Creations

If you have a strong online presence, you can monetize your content through various channels:

- YouTube: Earn through ads, sponsorships, and merchandise related to your content.
- Podcasting: Attract sponsors for your podcast episodes and offer premium content to subscribers.

17. Stock Photography: Monetize Your Photos

If you're a skilled photographer, you can earn income by selling your photos on stock photography websites.

18. Personal Training: Fitness and Wellness

Certify as a personal trainer and offer fitness training services to individuals or groups in your community or online.

19. Rent Your Assets: Utilize What You Have

If you have assets like equipment, tools, or vehicles that you don't use all the time, consider renting them out to others.

20. Consulting: Share Your Expertise

If you have specialized knowledge in a particular industry or field, offer consulting services to individuals or businesses seeking your insights.

21. Event Planning: Celebrations and Gatherings

Utilize your organizational skills to plan and execute events, such as parties, weddings, or corporate gatherings.

22. Language Translation: Linguistic Skills

If you're fluent in multiple languages, offer translation services for documents, websites, or communications.

23. Online Surveys and Market Research: Earn for Your Opinions

Participate in online surveys and market research studies to earn extra income by sharing your opinions.

24. Mystery Shopping: Evaluate Customer Experiences

Become a mystery shopper and get paid to visit stores, restaurants, or service providers to evaluate their customer experience.

25. Pet Sitting and Dog Walking: Animal Care Services

Offer pet sitting, dog walking, or pet care services for people who need assistance caring for their pets.

26. House Cleaning and Organizing: Domestic Services

Provide cleaning and organizing services for homes and businesses in your local area.

27. Virtual Assistance: Administrative Support

Offer virtual assistant services to busy professionals, entrepreneurs, or small businesses needing administrative support.

28. Car Detailing: Vehicle Cleaning and Maintenance

Provide car detailing services to individuals who want to keep their vehicles clean and well-maintained.

29. Property Management: Rental Property Services

If you have expertise in property management, offer your services to property owners who need assistance with maintenance, tenant interactions, and more.

30. Gardening and Landscaping: Green-Themed Services

If you have a green thumb, offer gardening and landscaping services to homeowners or businesses looking to enhance their outdoor spaces.

31. Online Coaching: Skills and Expertise
Offer coaching services in areas such as life, career, or business to help individuals reach their goals.

32. Crafting and Handmade Goods: Creative Ventures
If you're skilled in crafts, create handmade goods and sell them online or at local markets.

33. Specialty Cooking: Culinary Expertise

If you're a skilled cook or baker, offer catering, meal prep, or specialty baked goods to individuals or events.

34. Music Lessons: Share Your Musical Talent

If you're proficient in playing a musical instrument or singing, offer lessons to aspiring musicians.

35. Writing and Editing: Wordsmith Services

Utilize your writing and editing skills to offer content creation, copywriting, or editing services.

36. Repair and Maintenance Services: Handy Skills

If you're handy with tools, offer repair and maintenance services for home or vehicle-related issues.

37. Tech Support: IT Assistance

Offer tech support services to individuals or small businesses needing help with computer-related issues.

38. Tailoring and Alterations: Clothing Services

If you have sewing skills, offer tailoring and alteration services for clothing.

39. Language Tutoring: Teach Language Skills

Offer language tutoring services to individuals looking to learn or improve their language skills.

40. Event Photography: Capture Special Moments

If you're a skilled photographer, offer event photography services for weddings, parties, and other gatherings.

41. Health and Wellness Coaching: Fitness and Wellness

Utilize your knowledge of health and wellness to offer coaching services to individuals seeking a healthier lifestyle.

42. Financial Consulting: Money Management

If you have expertise in finance, offer consulting services to individuals or businesses seeking financial advice.

43. Home Staging: Real Estate Enhancement

Offer home staging services to individuals looking to sell their homes, enhancing the appeal of the property.

44. Teaching and Tutoring: Educational Assistance

If you're knowledgeable in a particular subject, offer tutoring or teaching services to students.

45. Personal Shopping: Shopping Assistance

Assist busy individuals or those seeking fashion advice by offering personal shopping services.

46. Car Repair and Maintenance: Auto Services

If you have automotive expertise, offer car repair and maintenance services to individuals in need.

47. Life Coaching: Personal Growth and Development

Offer life coaching services to individuals looking to set and achieve personal or professional goals.

48. Travel Planning: Vacation and Trip Assistance

Utilize your travel expertise to offer travel planning services to individuals or groups.

49. Beauty and Makeup Services: Enhance Appearances

If you're skilled in makeup application and beauty services, offer these services for special occasions or events.

50. Home Organizing: Clutter-Free Living

Offer home organizing services to individuals or families looking to declutter and organize their living spaces.

51. Tax Preparation: Financial Assistance

If you have knowledge of tax laws and regulations, offer tax preparation services to individuals and businesses.

52. Proofreading and Editing: Written Content Enhancement

Utilize your language skills to offer proofreading and editing services for written content.

53. Feng Shui Consulting: Harmonious Spaces

Offer feng shui consulting services to individuals seeking to create balanced and harmonious living spaces.

54. Car Washing and Detailing: Vehicle Care

Offer car washing and detailing services to individuals looking to keep their vehicles clean and well-maintained.

55. Art Classes: Creative Instruction

If you're skilled in art, offer art classes to individuals interested in learning and improving their artistic abilities.

56. Dance Classes: Movement Instruction

Utilize your dance skills to offer dance classes for individuals interested in learning various dance styles.

57. Yoga Instruction: Wellness Guidance

If you're a certified yoga instructor, offer yoga classes for individuals seeking physical and mental wellness.

58. House Painting: Home Improvement

Utilize your painting skills to offer house painting services to individuals looking to refresh their living spaces.

59. Nutrition Coaching: Dietary Guidance

Utilize your knowledge of nutrition to offer coaching services to individuals seeking healthier eating habits.

60. Pet Grooming: Animal Care Services

Offer pet grooming services to pet owners looking to keep their pets clean and well-groomed.

61. Event DJ: Entertainment Services

If you have DJ skills, offer your services for events such as weddings, parties, and gatherings.

62. Cleaning Services: Domestic Assistance
Offer cleaning services to individuals or businesses looking to maintain clean and organized spaces.

63. Voice Lessons: Vocal Training
If you have vocal skills, offer voice lessons to individuals interested in improving their singing abilities.

64. Online Marketing: Digital Promotion
Utilize your knowledge of online marketing to offer services like social media management, content creation, or digital advertising.

65. Interior Design: Space Enhancement

Offer interior design services to individuals or businesses seeking to create aesthetically pleasing and functional spaces.

66. Wedding Planning: Special Occasion Organization

Utilize your organizational skills to offer wedding planning services to couples planning their special day.

67. Language Interpreting: Linguistic Assistance

Utilize your language skills to offer interpretation services for individuals or businesses in need.

68. Handyman Services: General Repairs

If you're skilled in general repairs and maintenance, offer handyman services to individuals or businesses.

69. Childcare Services: Child Supervision

Offer childcare services to parents looking for reliable and trustworthy care for their children.

70. Virtual Event Planning: Remote Organization

Utilize your event planning skills to offer virtual event planning services for online gatherings and conferences.

71. Product Photography: Commercial Imaging

If you're a skilled photographer, offer product photography services for businesses looking to showcase their products.

72. Home Inspection: Property Assessment

If you have expertise in real estate or construction, offer home inspection services for potential buyers.

73. Social Media Management: Online Presence

Utilize your knowledge of social media platforms to offer management services for individuals or businesses.

74. Data Entry: Administrative Support

Offer data entry services to businesses in need of assistance with organizing and inputting data.

75. Online Therapy: Mental Health Support

If you're a licensed therapist, offer online therapy services to individuals seeking mental health support.

76. Mobile App Development: Digital Creation

If you have programming skills, offer mobile app development services for individuals or businesses.

77. Videography: Visual Storytelling

If you're a skilled videographer, offer videography services for events, businesses, or creative projects.

78. Handyman Services: General Repairs

If you're skilled in general repairs and maintenance, offer handyman services to individuals or businesses.

79. Language Teaching: Linguistic Instruction

Utilize your language skills to offer language teaching services to individuals interested in learning a new language.

80. Dog Training: Animal Behavior

If you have expertise in dog training, offer services to pet owners looking to train their dogs.

81. Online Fitness Classes: Virtual Workouts

Utilize your fitness expertise to offer online fitness classes for individuals seeking to exercise at home.

82. Personal Styling: Fashion Assistance

Offer personal styling services to individuals looking to enhance their wardrobe and appearance.

83. Public Speaking Coaching: Communication Skills

Utilize your public speaking skills to offer coaching to individuals looking to improve their communication abilities.

84. Home Renovation: Property Enhancement

Utilize your renovation skills to offer home renovation services to individuals looking to upgrade their living spaces.

85. Voiceover Services: Vocal Recording

If you have a distinctive voice, offer voiceover services for commercials, animations, and more.

86. Computer Repair: Tech Support

Utilize your tech skills to offer computer repair services for individuals or businesses.

87. Online Language Lessons: Virtual Instruction

Utilize your language skills to offer online language lessons to individuals interested in learning a new language.

88. Digital Marketing Consulting: Online Strategy

Utilize your expertise in digital marketing to offer consulting services to businesses seeking online visibility.

89. Car Rental: Vehicle Sharing

Utilize your available vehicles to offer car rental services to individuals in need of temporary transportation.

90. Resume Writing: Professional Development

Utilize your writing skills to offer resume writing services for individuals seeking to improve their job prospects.

91. Dance Instruction: Movement Teaching

Utilize your dance skills to offer dance instruction for individuals interested in learning various dance styles.

92. Party Planning: Event Organization

Utilize your organizational skills to offer party planning services for special occasions and celebrations.

93. Graphic Design: Visual Creation

If you're skilled in graphic design, offer design services for businesses in need of branding and marketing materials.

94. Content Editing: Document Enhancement

Utilize your language skills to offer content editing services for written materials.

95. Language Transcription: Audio-to-Text Conversion

Utilize your language skills to offer transcription services, converting audio content to written text.

96. Landscape Design: Outdoor Planning

Utilize your design skills to offer landscape design services for individuals or businesses looking to enhance their outdoor spaces.

97. Makeup Artistry: Beauty Services

If you're skilled in makeup application, offer makeup artistry services for special occasions or events.

98. Car Mechanic: Auto Repairs

Utilize your automotive expertise to offer car mechanic services for individuals in need of vehicle repairs.

99. Online Tutoring: Virtual Instruction

Utilize your expertise in a particular subject to offer online tutoring services to students.

100. Tour Guiding: Local Exploration

If you're knowledgeable about your area, offer tour guiding services for individuals looking to explore local attractions.

101. Online Surveys: Market Research

Participate in online surveys to earn extra income by sharing your opinions on various products and services.

102. Fitness Coaching: Physical Training

Utilize your fitness expertise to offer fitness coaching services for individuals seeking to achieve their health goals.

Traditional Employment vs. Entrepreneurship

The choice between traditional employment and entrepreneurship is a fundamental decision that shapes not only your career but also your lifestyle and financial trajectory. Each path has its merits, challenges, and considerations. Understanding the differences between traditional employment and entrepreneurship can help you make an informed choice aligned with your goals and aspirations.

Traditional Employment: Stability and Specialization

Pros:

- Stability: Traditional employment offers a consistent income stream, often with benefits like health insurance, retirement plans, and paid time off. This stability can provide a sense of financial security.
- Predictable Schedule: Many traditional jobs come with set working hours and a clear separation between work and personal life, allowing for more predictable routines.
- Skill Refinement: Traditional employment can provide an opportunity to specialize in a specific

role or field, allowing you to hone your skills and become an expert in your domain.

- Limited Risk: As an employee, you're shielded from the financial risks and responsibilities that entrepreneurs face, such as business failures and investment losses.

Cons:

- Limited Control: Employees often have limited control over decision-making, company direction, and the tasks they work on.
- Income Ceiling: Traditional employment can come with income limitations, such as fixed salaries and limited opportunities for significant earning growth.

- Dependency: Your career growth and income are tied to your employer's success and decisions, which can limit your autonomy.
- Less Flexibility: Traditional jobs may offer less flexibility in terms of work hours, location, and creative expression.

Entrepreneurship: Innovation and Autonomy

Pros:

- Autonomy: Entrepreneurs have the freedom to make decisions, shape their business vision, and drive their endeavors in the direction they desire.
- Unlimited Earning Potential: Successful entrepreneurship can lead

to substantial financial rewards, as your income isn't capped by a salary structure.

- Creativity and Innovation: Entrepreneurs have the opportunity to innovate, create new products or services, and contribute to industries in unique ways.

- Flexibility: Entrepreneurship often allows for flexibility in work hours, location, and balancing personal and professional life.

Cons:

- Financial Risk: Entrepreneurship comes with financial uncertainty and the risk of business failure. Investment of time, money, and resources is required, with no guaranteed return.

- Responsibility: Entrepreneurs bear the responsibility for all aspects of their business, from operations and finances to marketing and customer relations.
- Work-Life Balance: The pursuit of entrepreneurship can be all-consuming, potentially affecting work-life balance and personal time.
- Skill Diversity: Entrepreneurs need to wear multiple hats and be skilled in various areas, from product development to sales and marketing.

Choosing Your Path: Considerations

- Goals and Values: Clarify your long-term goals and personal values. Do you prioritize stability and a clear career path, or do you seek autonomy and the thrill of building something from scratch?

- Risk Tolerance: Assess your willingness to take on financial risks. Are you comfortable with the uncertainty that entrepreneurship entails, or do you prefer the security of a consistent paycheck?

- Skills and Passion: Consider your skills, expertise, and areas of passion. Do you want to specialize in a particular field or explore multiple areas by launching your own venture?

- Lifestyle: Reflect on the lifestyle you want. Are you willing to invest extensive hours and effort into entrepreneurship, or do you prefer a more structured work-life balance?

- Market and Industry: Research the market and industry you're interested in. Is there a demand for your product or service, and how competitive is the landscape?

- Support System: Consider your support system, including mentors, advisors, and potential partners. Do you have a network that can guide and assist you in your chosen path?

The decision between traditional employment and entrepreneurship is deeply personal and should align with your unique circumstances and aspirations. There's no one-size-fits-all answer—both paths have their merits and challenges. Some individuals find fulfillment in the stability and specialization of traditional employment, while others thrive on the innovation and autonomy of entrepreneurship. Whichever path you choose, thoughtful consideration and a clear understanding of your goals will guide you toward a fulfilling and successful career journey.

Passive Income Ventures: Real Estate, Investments, and More

Passive income has the power to transform your financial landscape by providing a consistent stream of earnings while allowing you to maintain a more flexible lifestyle. Passive income ventures involve upfront effort and investment, but they can generate ongoing returns that contribute to your financial freedom. Among the various avenues for generating passive income, real estate and investments stand out as key players. Let's explore these and other passive income opportunities that can help you build wealth over time.

1. Real Estate Investments: Building on Property

Real estate is a cornerstone of passive income generation, offering multiple avenues for earning without constant active involvement.

- Rental Properties: Invest in residential or commercial properties and earn rental income from tenants. This income can cover mortgage payments and expenses, leaving you with positive cash flow.

- Real Estate Investment Trusts (REITs): Invest in REITs, which allow you to pool resources with other investors to invest in a diversified portfolio of real estate properties. REITs often pay dividends based on rental income and property appreciation.

- Real Estate Crowdfunding: Participate in real estate projects with lower entry barriers through crowdfunding platforms. These projects can include rental properties, commercial developments, and more.

2. Dividend Stocks: Earning from Ownership

- Dividend stocks provide a way to earn a share of a company's profits as dividends, adding to your income without the need for active management.

- Dividend-Paying Stocks: Invest in established companies that distribute dividends regularly. These dividends can be reinvested for compound growth or used as additional income.

3. Peer-to-Peer Lending: Earning from Loans

- Peer-to-peer lending platforms connect borrowers with individual lenders, allowing you to earn interest by lending money to individuals or small businesses.

- Lending Platforms: Invest in loans across various risk profiles and earn interest over the loan term.

4. Bond Investments: Fixed Income Returns

- Bonds are debt securities issued by governments or corporations, offering fixed interest payments over a specified period.

- Corporate Bonds: Invest in bonds issued by corporations, earning interest as fixed income.
- Government Bonds: Invest in bonds issued by governments, providing a secure investment option with predictable returns.

5. Automated Online Businesses: Digital Income Streams

- Online businesses can be automated to generate passive income, utilizing technology and systems to minimize active involvement.
- E-commerce Stores: Set up online stores that utilize dropshipping or print-on-demand services to fulfill orders and generate income.
- Affiliate Marketing: Create content or websites that promote products and

earn commissions for every sale made through your referral.

6. Royalties and Licensing: Intellectual Property Income

- If you create intellectual property, such as books, music, or software, you can earn royalties from the use or licensing of your creations.

- Books and E-books: Publish books or e-books and earn royalties from each sale.

- Music and Art: License your music compositions or art for use in various media.

7. Automated Investment Platforms: Robo-Advisors

- Robo-advisors are automated investment platforms that use

algorithms to manage and rebalance your investment portfolio.

- Automated Diversification: Invest in a diversified portfolio of stocks and bonds, managed by algorithms to optimize returns and risk.

8. High-Yield Savings Accounts: Interest Earnings

- High-yield savings accounts offer competitive interest rates, allowing your savings to grow over time.

- Interest Earnings: Park your funds in a high-yield savings account and earn interest on your balance.

9. Renting Assets: Sharing Economy Income

- Utilize the sharing economy to rent out assets you already own, generating income from items you may not use constantly.

- Car Rentals: Rent out your car when you're not using it through platforms like Turo.
- Home Rentals: Rent out a spare room or your entire home on platforms like Airbnb.

10. Licensing Your Ideas: Intellectual Ventures

- If you have innovative ideas, you can license them to companies for commercialization.
- Patents: License your patented inventions to companies for manufacturing and distribution.
- Product Designs: Sell your product designs to manufacturers or retailers.

11. Blogging and Content Creation: Digital Revenue Streams

- Create valuable content on platforms like blogs or YouTube channels, and monetize through ads, sponsorships, and merchandise.
- Ad Revenue: Earn income from ads displayed on your content.
- Sponsorships: Partner with brands for sponsored content.

12. Stock Photography: Selling Visual Assets

- If you're a skilled photographer, sell your photos on stock photography websites.
- Visual Licensing: Sell your photographs for use in various media.

13. Online Courses and E-learning: Knowledge Monetization

- Create and sell online courses on platforms like Udemy or Teachable, sharing your expertise and knowledge.
- Course Sales: Earn income from course enrollments.

14. Automatic Investment: Dollar-Cost Averaging

- Invest a fixed amount of money at regular intervals, taking advantage of market fluctuations.
- Regular Investments: Invest a consistent amount in the market, potentially benefiting from the average cost of your investments over time.

15. Automated Dropshipping: E-commerce Without Inventory

- Set up an e-commerce store that utilizes dropshipping, where the products are shipped directly from the supplier to the customer.
- Order Fulfillment: When a customer orders a product, the supplier handles the shipping, eliminating the need for inventory management.

16. Self-Publishing: Authoring Your Success

- Write and self-publish books, e-books, or guides to earn royalties from sales.
- Direct Publishing: Self-publish your content on platforms like Amazon Kindle Direct Publishing.

17. ATM Ownership: Passive Cash Flow

- Invest in ATMs and earn a portion of the fees collected from each transaction.

- Cash Flow: Generate passive income from ATM transaction fees.

18. App Development: Digital Products

- Develop and launch mobile apps that generate income through downloads, in-app purchases, or subscriptions.
- App Revenue: Earn income from app downloads and in-app purchases.

19. Music Streaming: Digital Royalties

- If you're a musician, earn royalties from your music being streamed on platforms like Spotify.
- Streaming Royalties: Earn income based on the number of times your music is streamed.

20. Intellectual Property: Monetizing Creativity

- If you're a designer or artist, license your designs and creative works for commercial use.
- Design Licensing: Earn income from the use of your designs in various products.

Choosing Your Passive Income Ventures: Considerations

- Interests and Skills: Choose ventures that align with your interests and skills to ensure sustained engagement.
- Risk Tolerance: Assess the level of risk associated with each venture and determine what aligns with your risk tolerance.
- Investment: Consider the initial investment required for each venture and match it with your available resources.

- Time Commitment: Evaluate the time required for setup, maintenance, and management of each income stream.
- Diversification: Consider diversifying your passive income sources to mitigate risks and maximize potential returns.
- Long-Term Viability: Assess the long-term viability of the venture, ensuring it can generate sustainable income over time.
- Market Demand: Research market demand and competition for the chosen venture to ensure a viable income stream.

Passive income ventures offer a pathway to financial independence, allowing you to generate income with less day-to-day involvement compared to traditional employment. Diversification, careful planning, and a clear understanding of your chosen ventures are essential for success. Whether you're investing in real estate, generating royalties from intellectual property, or exploring other avenues, building a well-balanced and diversified passive income portfolio can set you on a journey toward financial freedom and the lifestyle you desire.

The Power of Compounding and Investment

One of the most remarkable concepts in the world of finance is the power of compounding. When combined with strategic investment, it has the potential to turn even modest contributions into substantial wealth over time. Understanding how compounding works and harnessing its force through smart investment decisions can significantly impact your financial journey. Let's delve into the mechanics of compounding and how it fuels the growth of your investments.

The Magic of Compounding: A Snowball Effect

At its core, compounding is the process of earning interest or returns on an initial investment, and then reinvesting those earnings to generate additional returns. Over time, this cycle of reinvestment accelerates the growth of your money, creating a snowball effect that leads to exponential growth. Here's how it works:

- Initial Investment: You start by investing a certain amount of money, whether it's in a savings account, stocks, bonds, or other assets.
- Earning Returns: As time goes by, your investment earns returns. These returns can come in the form of

interest, dividends, capital gains, or any other type of profit.

- Reinvestment: Instead of withdrawing the earnings, you reinvest them back into the same investment. This increases your investment base, and now your future returns are based on the larger amount.

- Compounding Effect: With each reinvestment, your investment base grows, and your returns become larger. This compounding effect continues to build upon itself, leading to exponential growth.

The Role of Time: Key to Maximizing Compounding

The most significant factor in the power of compounding is time. The longer your money has to compound, the more dramatic the effects become. This is why starting to invest early in life is often emphasized as a crucial financial strategy. Even small contributions made consistently over a long period can result in substantial wealth due to the prolonged compounding process.

Investment Vehicles for Compounding Growth

Several investment vehicles can harness the power of compounding to help you grow your wealth over time:

- Stock Market: Investing in stocks allows you to participate in the growth of companies over the long term. Through capital appreciation and dividends, your investment can compound significantly.

- Mutual Funds and ETFs: These funds pool money from multiple investors to invest in a diversified portfolio of stocks, bonds, or other assets. They offer a convenient way to benefit from compounding even with smaller initial investments.
- Retirement Accounts (e.g., 401(k) and IRAs): Retirement accounts offer tax advantages and can be powerful tools for compounding. Contributions and earnings grow tax-deferred or tax-free, allowing your money to compound more effectively.
- Real Estate: Real estate investment, particularly rental properties, can generate rental income and property appreciation, both of which contribute to compounding growth.

- Bonds: Bonds provide interest payments, and when those interest payments are reinvested, they contribute to compounding growth.

Harnessing the Power: Tips for Effective Compounding

- Start Early: The earlier you begin investing, the longer your money has to compound. Even if you start with small amounts, consistent contributions over time can lead to significant growth.
- Consistency: Regular contributions, even if they're small, can make a big difference. Automate your investments to ensure consistency.
- Reinvest Earnings: Whenever your investments generate returns, reinvest

them to take full advantage of compounding.

- Diversification: Diversifying your investments helps manage risk while still allowing you to benefit from compounding across different assets.
- Long-Term Perspective: Understand that compounding is a long-term strategy. Avoid making emotional decisions based on short-term market fluctuations.
- Patience: Compounding takes time to yield significant results. Be patient and stay committed to your investment strategy.

Example: The Power of Time and Compounding

Let's illustrate the power of compounding with an example. Suppose you invest $10,000 in an investment that generates an average annual return of 8%. Without adding any additional funds, your investment will grow as follows:

After 10 years: $21,589
After 20 years: $46,609
After 30 years: $100,627
After 40 years: $217,254

In this example, you can see how the initial $10,000 investment grows significantly over time due to the effects of compounding. The longer you allow your money to compound, the more pronounced the growth becomes.

Compounding, fueled by strategic investment decisions, is a powerful ally on your journey to financial independence. By starting early, consistently contributing, and allowing time to work its magic, you can watch your investments grow far beyond your initial contributions. Understanding and harnessing the force of compounding can help you build a more secure and prosperous financial future.

Harnessing Compound Interest for Long-Term Growth

Compound interest is often referred to as the "eighth wonder of the world" due to its remarkable ability to multiply your wealth over time. By consistently reinvesting your earnings, compound interest can turn small contributions into substantial sums. Whether you're saving for retirement, a major purchase, or simply looking to build wealth, understanding and utilizing compound interest can be a game-changer. Let's explore how you can harness compound interest for long-term growth and financial security.

1. Start Early: The Power of Time

The most critical factor in the success of compound interest is time. Starting early gives your investments more time to grow and compound, magnifying the effects. Even if you're only able to invest small amounts initially, the longer your money has to work, the greater the impact on your wealth.

2. Consistent Contributions: The Building Blocks

Regular and consistent contributions are the building blocks of effective compound interest. Whether it's a monthly or annual investment, committing to a routine contribution schedule helps maximize growth. Even if your contributions are modest, the consistent flow of money compounds over time.

3. Reinvest Earnings: Fueling the Cycle

Reinvesting the earnings from your investments is the key to unleashing the true power of compound interest. Instead of withdrawing your gains, let them stay in the investment to generate more returns. This creates a compounding cycle where your earnings earn even more earnings.

4. Choose the Right Investments: Growth Matters

Investments that generate compounding growth are crucial. Stocks, bonds, mutual funds, and retirement accounts are common options. Stocks tend to offer higher growth potential, while bonds provide stability. Diversification can help balance risk and reward.

5. Understand the Rule of 72: Quick Estimation

The Rule of 72 is a simple formula to estimate how long it takes for your money to double based on a fixed annual rate of return. Divide 72 by the annual interest rate, and you'll get an approximate number of years it takes for your investment to double.

6. Stay Patient: Long-Term Perspective

Compound interest is most effective when viewed over the long term. Avoid the temptation to make impulsive decisions based on short-term market fluctuations. Stay patient and let the compounding process work its magic.

7. Visualize the Long-Term Impact: Seeing Is Believing

Seeing the potential impact of compound interest can be inspiring. Use online compound interest calculators to project how your investments might grow over time based on different contribution amounts, interest rates, and timeframes.

Example: Compound Interest in Action

Let's illustrate with an example: Suppose you invest $5,000 in a retirement account at age 25. You consistently contribute $200 per month, and your investments generate an average annual return of 7%. Here's how your investment could grow:

After 10 years: $34,615
After 20 years: $110,890

After 30 years: $278,122

After 40 years: $593,713

In this example, you can see how compound interest, combined with consistent contributions, transforms an initial investment into a substantial sum over time.

Harnessing compound interest for long-term growth is a strategic approach to securing your financial future. By starting early, making consistent contributions, reinvesting earnings, and maintaining a patient outlook, you can leverage the power of compounding to your advantage. No matter your current financial situation, taking steps to integrate compound interest into your wealth-building strategy can set you on a path toward achieving your financial goals and enjoying the benefits of a secure and prosperous future.

Understanding Different Investment Vehicles

Investing is a key pathway to building wealth over time, and there are various investment vehicles available to help you achieve your financial goals. Each investment vehicle has its own characteristics, risk profile, and potential returns. Understanding these options will empower you to make informed decisions that align with your investment objectives and risk tolerance. Let's explore some of the most common investment vehicles:

1. Stocks: Ownership in Companies

Investing in stocks means buying shares of ownership in a company. Stocks offer the potential for high returns but also come with higher volatility.

- Pros: Potential for capital appreciation, dividends, ownership in companies with growth potential.
- Cons: Higher risk due to market fluctuations, potential for losses.

2. Bonds: Fixed-Income Securities

Bonds are debt securities issued by governments or corporations. When you invest in bonds, you're essentially lending money in exchange for periodic interest payments and the return of the principal amount at maturity.

- Pros: Generally lower risk compared to stocks, regular interest income.
- Cons: Lower potential for capital appreciation, interest rate risk.

3. Mutual Funds: Diversified Portfolios

Mutual funds pool money from multiple investors to invest in a diversified portfolio of stocks, bonds, or other assets. They offer diversification without requiring you to select individual securities.

- Pros: Diversification, professional management, accessibility.
- Cons: Management fees, potential for capital gains tax.

4. Exchange-Traded Funds (ETFs): Flexible Investing

ETFs are similar to mutual funds but trade on stock exchanges like individual stocks. They offer exposure to various asset classes, sectors, and markets.

- Pros: Diversification, lower expense ratios, flexibility.

- Cons: Brokerage commissions, potential for capital gains tax.

5. Real Estate: Property Investments

Investing in real estate involves purchasing property with the expectation of earning rental income and potential property appreciation.

- Pros: Rental income, potential for property appreciation, tangible asset.
- Cons: Property management, illiquidity.

6. Retirement Accounts: Long-Term Planning

Retirement accounts like 401(k)s and IRAs offer tax advantages for long-term savings. They often include options to invest in stocks, bonds, and mutual funds.

- Pros: Tax advantages, long-term growth potential.
- Cons: Early withdrawal penalties, contribution limits.

7. Commodities: Tangible Assets

Commodities include physical assets like gold, silver, oil, and agricultural products. Investing in commodities can provide a hedge against inflation.

- Pros: Hedge against inflation, portfolio diversification.
- Cons: Volatility, storage costs for physical commodities.

8. Certificates of Deposit (CDs): Fixed-Term Deposits

CDs are time deposits offered by banks with a fixed term and fixed interest rate. They are considered lower-risk investments.

- Pros: Fixed interest rates, FDIC-insured (up to limits).
- Cons: Limited liquidity, lower potential returns.

9. Options and Derivatives: Complex Strategies

Options and derivatives are more complex investment tools that involve contracts based on the value of underlying assets like stocks or commodities.

- Pros: Hedging strategies, potential for leverage.
- Cons: Complex, higher risk, potential for losses.

10. Money Market Funds: Short-Term Investments

Money market funds invest in short-term, low-risk securities like government bonds and commercial paper. They are considered relatively safe.

- Pros: Low risk, liquidity.
- Cons: Low potential returns.

11. Annuities: Retirement Income

Annuities are insurance products that provide regular payments over a specified period or for life. They are often used as retirement income solutions.

- Pros: Guaranteed income, tax-deferral benefits.
- Cons: Fees, potential lack of liquidity.

12. Savings Accounts: Basic Savings

Savings accounts are offered by banks and provide a safe place to store funds while earning interest.

- Pros: Liquidity, safety.

- Cons: Low interest rates, limited growth.

Choosing the Right Investment Vehicles: Considerations

- Risk Tolerance: Assess your comfort level with risk. Some investments offer higher returns but come with greater volatility.

- Investment Goals: Define your objectives—whether it's capital appreciation, income generation, or long-term growth.

- Time Horizon: Consider your investment horizon. Some investments are better suited for short-term goals, while others are designed for long-term growth.

- Diversification: Spreading your investments across different asset classes can help manage risk and optimize returns.
- Research: Understand the characteristics and historical performance of each investment vehicle before investing.
- Professional Advice: Consider consulting a financial advisor to create a customized investment strategy aligned with your goals and risk tolerance.

Each investment vehicle has its own set of advantages and drawbacks. Building a diversified investment portfolio that aligns with your financial goals and risk tolerance is a key step toward achieving long-term success. By understanding these different options, you can make informed decisions that contribute to your financial growth and security over time.

Risk Management and Wealth Protection

While investing offers the potential for wealth growth, it's important to recognize that all investments come with a certain level of risk. Risk management is a crucial aspect of any financial strategy, as it helps protect your hard-earned wealth from potential losses. By implementing effective risk management practices, you can safeguard your financial future and make informed decisions that balance potential rewards with potential risks. Let's explore key principles of risk management and strategies to protect your wealth.

1. Understand Your Risk Tolerance

Risk tolerance refers to your comfort level with the ups and downs of investing. Assess your willingness and ability to endure market fluctuations without making impulsive decisions. Your risk tolerance will influence your investment choices and asset allocation.

2. Diversification: Spreading Risk

Diversification involves spreading your investments across different asset classes, industries, and geographic regions. This helps reduce the impact of poor performance in any single investment. By diversifying, you avoid putting all your eggs in one basket.

3. Asset Allocation: Balancing Risk and Reward

Determining how much of your portfolio should be allocated to different asset classes (such as stocks, bonds, and cash) is a crucial decision. Asset allocation aims to balance risk and reward based on your investment goals, time horizon, and risk tolerance.

4. Emergency Fund: Financial Safety Net

Maintain an emergency fund with enough funds to cover unexpected expenses, such as medical bills or job loss. This prevents you from liquidating investments prematurely during times of need.

5. Insurance: Protecting Against Losses

Insurance serves as a safety net to protect against unforeseen events. Health insurance, auto insurance, home insurance, and life insurance provide financial support in times of crisis.

6. Long-Term Perspective: Riding Out Market Volatility

Market fluctuations are inevitable. A long-term perspective allows you to withstand short-term volatility with the confidence that your investments can recover and grow over time.

7. Risk Assessment: Evaluating Investments

Thoroughly research and understand the risks associated with each investment before committing funds. Assess factors like historical performance, market trends, and economic conditions.

8. Regular Review: Stay Informed

Regularly review your investment portfolio and financial goals. As your circumstances change, your risk tolerance and investment strategy may need adjustment.

9. Dollar-Cost Averaging: Consistent Investing

Dollar-cost averaging involves investing a fixed amount at regular intervals, regardless of market conditions. This strategy reduces the impact of market volatility and allows you to buy more shares when prices are low and fewer shares when prices are high.

10. Professional Guidance: Financial Advisors

Consulting a qualified financial advisor can provide valuable insights into risk management strategies tailored to your specific situation and goals.

11. Limit Speculation: Avoid Chasing Trends
Speculative investments, such as day trading or chasing market trends, can expose you to higher risk. Stick to a disciplined investment strategy aligned with your long-term goals.

12. Understand Investment Products: Avoid Complexities
Avoid investments with complex structures that you don't fully understand. Complicated investments often come with hidden risks.

13. Regular Monitoring: Stay Vigilant
Stay informed about market trends, economic indicators, and geopolitical

developments that could impact your investments.

14. Minimize Debt: Reduce Financial Stress
Manage and reduce high-interest debt. High debt levels can increase financial stress and limit your ability to weather economic downturns.

15. Stay Educated: Knowledge Is Key
Continuously educate yourself about investment principles, economic trends, and financial best practices. Informed decisions are the foundation of effective risk management.

Risk management is an integral part of securing your financial well-being. By understanding your risk tolerance, diversifying your investments, maintaining an emergency fund, and staying informed, you can navigate the uncertainties of the financial world with confidence. A combination of strategic planning, long-term perspective, and sound financial advice can help you protect your wealth and achieve your financial goals, even in the face of economic challenges.

Insurance: Safeguarding Your Financial Future

Insurance plays a crucial role in safeguarding your financial well-being by providing a safety net against unexpected events that could lead to financial loss. From health crises to property damage, insurance offers peace of mind by transferring the financial risks associated with these events to an insurance provider. Understanding the types of insurance available and their benefits will help you make informed decisions to protect yourself, your loved ones, and your assets.

1. Health Insurance: Vital Coverage

Health insurance covers medical expenses, including doctor visits, hospital stays, prescription medications, and preventive care. It helps you manage the potentially high costs of medical treatments while ensuring access to quality healthcare.

2. Auto Insurance: On the Road to Protection

Auto insurance provides coverage for vehicle-related accidents, damages, and injuries. It's not only a legal requirement in many places but also essential for protecting your vehicle and your financial assets in case of accidents.

3. Homeowners or Renters Insurance: Sheltering Your Assets

Homeowners insurance covers damage to your home and personal property due to various perils, such as fire, theft, and natural disasters. Renters insurance offers similar coverage for personal belongings within a rented property.

4. Life Insurance: Providing for Loved Ones
Life insurance offers financial protection for your loved ones in the event of your death. It can help cover funeral expenses, outstanding debts, and provide income replacement for your family.

5. Disability Insurance: Protecting Your Earnings
Disability insurance replaces a portion of your income if you're unable to work due to a disability or illness. It ensures you can continue meeting your financial obligations even if you're unable to work temporarily or long-term.

6. Long-Term Care Insurance: Planning for the Future

Long-term care insurance covers costs associated with assisted living, nursing home care, and in-home care services for individuals who need assistance with daily activities due to aging or health issues.

7. Umbrella Insurance: Extra Layer of Protection

Umbrella insurance provides additional liability coverage beyond the limits of your auto, home, or renters insurance. It's designed to protect you from significant financial losses resulting from lawsuits or claims.

8. Travel Insurance: Ensuring Safe Journeys

Travel insurance offers coverage for trip cancellations, medical emergencies, lost baggage, and other unforeseen events during your travels.

9. Business Insurance: Protecting Business Assets

Business insurance covers risks specific to your business, including property damage, liability, and employee-related issues. It ensures the continuity of your business operations despite unexpected setbacks.

10. Pet Insurance: Caring for Your Furry Friends

Pet insurance covers veterinary expenses for your pets, helping you manage the costs of medical treatments and procedures.

Choosing the Right Insurance: Considerations

- Assess Your Needs: Evaluate your personal and financial situation to determine the types of insurance that best fit your needs. Consider your family size, lifestyle, assets, and potential risks.

- Understand Coverage: Read policy terms carefully to understand what is covered, excluded, and the limits of coverage. Be aware of deductibles, co-payments, and coverage restrictions.

- Compare Policies: Shop around and obtain quotes from multiple insurance providers to compare coverage options and costs.

- Seek Professional Advice: Consider consulting an insurance agent or financial advisor to help you understand your insurance needs and make informed decisions.
- Review Regularly: As your life circumstances change, update your insurance coverage to ensure it remains aligned with your current needs.
- Bundle Policies: Some insurance companies offer discounts when you bundle multiple policies, such as auto and home insurance.

Insurance is a vital tool for protecting your financial future from unexpected events that can lead to significant financial losses. By understanding your insurance needs, researching coverage options, and choosing policies that align with your circumstances, you can build a comprehensive safety net that provides you and your loved ones with peace of mind and financial security.

Mitigating Investment Risks and Market Volatility

Investing in the financial markets offers the potential for significant returns, but it also comes with inherent risks and market volatility. To safeguard your investments and financial well-being, it's essential to adopt strategies that help mitigate these risks and navigate the ups and downs of the market. By following proven risk management practices and maintaining a disciplined approach, you can minimize the impact of market volatility and work towards achieving your long-term financial goals.

1. Diversification: Your Defense Against Volatility

Diversification involves spreading your investments across different asset classes, industries, and geographic regions. This helps reduce the impact of poor performance in any single investment. By holding a mix of assets, you can potentially offset losses in one area with gains in another.

2. Asset Allocation: Tailoring Your Portfolio

Strategic asset allocation involves determining the right mix of assets for your investment portfolio based on your financial goals, risk tolerance, and investment horizon. Adjusting your allocation as you age and your circumstances change can help manage risk.

3. Long-Term Perspective: Riding Out Storms

Adopting a long-term investment horizon can help you ride out market fluctuations. Historically, markets have experienced both ups and downs, but over the long term, they tend to trend upward.

4. Dollar-Cost Averaging: Consistency Amid Volatility

Investing a fixed amount at regular intervals, regardless of market conditions, is known as dollar-cost averaging. This strategy allows you to buy more shares when prices are low and fewer shares when prices are high, potentially reducing the impact of market volatility.

5. Stay Informed: Knowledge as a Shield

Stay informed about market trends, economic indicators, and geopolitical developments. Knowledge empowers you to make informed decisions rather than react emotionally to market fluctuations.

6. Avoid Emotional Decisions: Discipline is Key

Emotional reactions to market volatility can lead to impulsive decisions that harm your long-term financial goals. Maintain a disciplined approach and avoid making drastic changes based on short-term fluctuations.

7. Emergency Fund: Protecting Investments
Maintaining an emergency fund ensures you have liquid funds available to cover unexpected expenses. This prevents you from selling investments at unfavorable times to meet immediate financial needs.

8. Review and Rebalance: Stay Aligned
Regularly review your investment portfolio and rebalance it as needed to ensure it remains aligned with your target asset allocation. Rebalancing can help you capitalize on market fluctuations.

9. Professional Advice: Seeking Expert Guidance
Consider consulting a financial advisor who can provide personalized advice based on

your financial goals, risk tolerance, and market conditions.

10. Limit Speculative Activities: Prudent Investing

Avoid speculative behaviors like day trading or chasing market trends, which can increase your exposure to unnecessary risk.

11. Understanding Risk Tolerance: Know Yourself

Be aware of your risk tolerance and invest accordingly. Investments should align with your comfort level and financial goals.

12. Investment Education: Building Confidence

Educate yourself about investment principles, market dynamics, and various investment vehicles. Knowledge builds confidence and helps you make informed decisions.

13. Hedging Strategies: Risk Reduction
Explore options for using hedging strategies, such as purchasing put options, to protect your investments against potential market downturns.

14. Consistency: Steadfast Approach
Consistency is key to successful investing. Stick to your investment plan, even during challenging market conditions.

15. Patience: The Power of Time
Remember that the effects of compounding and market recovery often take time.

Patience is essential for achieving long-term financial success.

Market volatility is an inherent part of investing, but with the right strategies, you can mitigate its impact and work towards your financial goals with confidence. By diversifying your investments, adopting a long-term perspective, staying informed, and avoiding emotional decisions, you can navigate the ups and downs of the market while positioning yourself for long-term financial stability and growth.

Real Estate as a Wealth-Building Tool

Real estate investment has long been recognized as a powerful wealth-building tool. With the potential for rental income, property appreciation, and various tax advantages, real estate offers unique opportunities for individuals looking to diversify their investment portfolio and achieve long-term financial success. Understanding the benefits and strategies associated with real estate investing can help you harness its potential to build wealth over time.

1. Rental Income: Generating Passive Cash Flow

Investing in rental properties allows you to generate consistent rental income. This passive cash flow can provide a steady stream of revenue to supplement your other income sources and cover property-related expenses.

2. Property Appreciation: Growing Your Investment

Real estate has the potential to appreciate in value over time. As demand for properties increases, their market value may rise, allowing you to sell the property at a profit. Property appreciation is a key factor in building long-term wealth through real estate.

3. Leverage: Maximizing Returns

Real estate allows you to use leverage by financing a portion of the property's purchase price through a mortgage. This enables you to control a valuable asset with a relatively small upfront investment, potentially magnifying your returns.

4. Tax Benefits: Saving Money

Real estate investors often enjoy tax advantages, including deductions for mortgage interest, property taxes, maintenance expenses, and depreciation. These deductions can significantly reduce your taxable income and increase your after-tax returns.

5. Hedge Against Inflation: Protecting Your Wealth

Real estate can serve as a hedge against inflation. As the cost of living rises, so can rental income and property values, helping you maintain your purchasing power over time.

6. Portfolio Diversification: Spreading Risk

Adding real estate to your investment portfolio diversifies your holdings, reducing risk exposure to fluctuations in the stock market. This diversification can enhance your overall portfolio stability.

7. Real Assets: Tangible Investments

Real estate investments are tangible assets, providing a sense of security and control.

Unlike stocks or bonds, you have direct ownership of a physical property.

8. Different Investment Strategies: Flexibility

Real estate offers various investment strategies, including residential rental properties, commercial properties, real estate investment trusts (REITs), and real estate crowdfunding. Choose the strategy that aligns with your goals and risk tolerance.

9. Active or Passive Investing: Your Choice

Real estate investing can be as hands-on or hands-off as you prefer. Active investors may choose to manage their properties, while passive investors can opt for real estate funds or partnerships.

10. Due Diligence: Research Matters

Thoroughly research potential properties, locations, and market trends before making an investment. Conduct due diligence to understand the potential risks and rewards.

11. Property Management: Efficiency and Scale

If you choose to invest in rental properties, consider whether to manage them yourself or hire a property management company. Effective property management ensures smooth operations and tenant satisfaction.

12. Risk Management: Preparedness

Like any investment, real estate carries risks, such as market downturns, property damage, and vacancy periods. Adequate risk management, such as maintaining an emergency fund and having a contingency plan, is crucial.

13. Long-Term Perspective: Patience Pays Off

Real estate is generally considered a long-term investment. Property values and rental income tend to appreciate gradually over time, rewarding patient investors.

14. Professional Advice: Expert Guidance

Seek advice from real estate professionals, financial advisors, and legal experts to ensure you make informed decisions that align with your financial goals.

Real estate investment offers a powerful pathway to building wealth, providing opportunities for rental income, property appreciation, and tax advantages. By conducting thorough research, diversifying your portfolio, and understanding the various investment strategies, you can unlock the potential of real estate as a valuable tool in your journey toward achieving financial success and security.

Real Estate Investment Strategies and Considerations

Real estate investment offers a range of strategies, each with its own benefits and challenges. Whether you're a seasoned investor or just starting, choosing the right strategy and understanding the associated considerations is essential for maximizing your returns and minimizing risks. Here are some prominent real estate investment strategies and factors to bear in mind as you build your real estate portfolio:

1. Buy and Hold: Long-Term Appreciation
The buy and hold strategy involves purchasing a property with the intention of holding onto it for an extended period, often years or even decades. This strategy

capitalizes on property appreciation over time, generating long-term wealth through a combination of rental income and increasing property values.

Considerations:

- Market Selection: Choose locations with strong growth potential and amenities that attract renters or buyers.
- Property Management: Decide whether you'll manage the property yourself or hire a property management company.
- Cash Flow Analysis: Ensure the property's rental income covers expenses like mortgage payments, maintenance, and property management costs.

2. Fix and Flip: Short-Term Profit

The fix and flip strategy involves purchasing distressed properties, renovating or improving them, and then selling them for a profit. This strategy requires a keen eye for properties with potential and a solid understanding of renovation costs.

Considerations:

- Renovation Costs: Accurately estimate the costs of renovations to avoid eroding your potential profits.
- Market Timing: Consider market conditions and demand for renovated properties in your chosen location.
- Resale Value: Research comparable sales to determine a competitive sale price for the renovated property.

3. Real Estate Investment Trusts (REITs): Passive Investing

REITs are companies that own, operate, or finance income-producing real estate across various sectors. By investing in REITs, you can gain exposure to real estate markets without direct property ownership. They offer liquidity and the potential for dividend income.

Considerations:

- Dividend Yields: Research the historical dividend yields and performance of REITs before investing.
- Sector Focus: Different REITs focus on various types of properties, such as residential, commercial, or industrial.

Choose based on your goals and risk tolerance.

- Market Conditions: Monitor how market conditions affect the performance of the REIT and its underlying properties.

4. Real Estate Crowdfunding: Collaborative Investing

Real estate crowdfunding platforms allow multiple investors to pool funds for projects, such as purchasing properties or development ventures. This strategy offers accessibility to real estate investments with lower minimum investment requirements.

Considerations:

- Platform Selection: Choose reputable crowdfunding platforms with a track record of successful projects.

- Project Analysis: Evaluate the details of each project, including the property's location, financial projections, and the platform's due diligence.
- Diversification: Spread your investments across multiple projects to reduce risk.

5. Vacation Rentals: Short-Term Income

Vacation rentals involve leasing out properties on a short-term basis to travelers. Platforms like Airbnb have made it easier for property owners to profit from the tourism industry.

Considerations:

- Regulations: Research local regulations regarding short-term rentals, as they can vary significantly.

- Location: Choose properties in desirable tourist destinations or areas with high demand for short-term rentals.
- Property Management: Consider whether you'll manage the property yourself or use a vacation rental management service.

6. Commercial Real Estate: Diversification and Income

Investing in commercial properties such as office buildings, retail spaces, or warehouses can provide steady rental income and the potential for long-term appreciation.

Considerations:

- Tenant Analysis: Evaluate the creditworthiness and stability of potential commercial tenants.

- Market Trends: Understand the demand for specific commercial property types in your chosen market.
- Lease Terms: Consider the length and terms of leases, which can impact your rental income stability.

7. Single-Family Rentals: Entry-Level Investment

Investing in single-family homes and renting them out can provide a steady stream of rental income. This strategy is often considered less complex than commercial real estate or large multi-unit properties.

Considerations:
- Property Location: Choose neighborhoods with strong demand

for rentals and favorable rental market conditions.

- Property Condition: Balance renovation costs with potential rental income and property value appreciation.
- Tenant Screening: Implement thorough tenant screening processes to minimize the risk of rental issues.

8. Tax Implications: Accounting for Taxes Understand the tax implications of your chosen strategy. Different strategies may have varying tax advantages or consequences, such as depreciation deductions for rental properties or capital gains taxes for property sales.

Each real estate investment strategy offers its own set of benefits and challenges. The key to success lies in aligning your strategy with your financial goals, risk tolerance, and expertise. Thorough research, due diligence, and a well-thought-out investment plan will help you navigate the real estate market and leverage its potential to build wealth over time. Whether you're interested in rental income, property appreciation, or a combination of both, understanding the nuances of each strategy is the first step toward achieving real estate investment success.

Rental Properties and Property Flipping

Rental properties and property flipping are two distinct real estate investment strategies, each offering unique opportunities and challenges. Whether you're interested in generating passive income through rental properties or seeking short-term profits through property flipping, understanding the intricacies of each strategy is crucial for making informed investment decisions and achieving success in the real estate market.

Rental Properties: Generating Passive Income

1. Strategy Overview:

Investing in rental properties involves purchasing residential or commercial properties with the intention of leasing them out to tenants. The primary goal is to generate consistent rental income while potentially benefiting from property appreciation over time.

Benefits:

- Steady Income: Rental properties provide a reliable source of passive income that can help cover mortgage payments and property expenses.
- Long-Term Wealth: Over time, property values can appreciate,

contributing to long-term wealth accumulation.

- Tax Benefits: Rental income can be offset by deductions for mortgage interest, property taxes, maintenance costs, and depreciation.

Challenges:

- Property Management: Effective property management is crucial for tenant satisfaction and minimizing vacancies.

- Tenant Relations: Dealing with tenant-related issues, such as late payments or property damage, requires careful management.

- Market Risks: Economic fluctuations and changing rental market conditions can impact rental income and property values.

Property Flipping: Seeking Short-Term Profits

1. Strategy Overview:

Property flipping involves purchasing distressed properties at a lower price, renovating or improving them, and selling them for a profit within a relatively short timeframe.

Benefits:

- Profit Potential: Successful property flipping can yield substantial short-term profits, especially in a rising market.
- Realization of Value: Property improvements can enhance the property's value and attract higher selling prices.

- Active Involvement: Property flipping allows for hands-on involvement in the transformation and sale of properties.

Challenges:

- Renovation Costs: Accurately estimating renovation costs is essential to ensure potential profits are not eroded.
- Market Timing: Fluctuations in the real estate market can impact demand and resale values.
- Risks of Overimprovement: Overinvesting in renovations can lead to diminishing returns and decreased profitability.

Factors to Consider:

1. Market Analysis:

Rental Properties: Choose markets with strong rental demand and potential for long-term appreciation.

Property Flipping: Consider market trends and the potential for short-term price appreciation.

2. Property Selection:

Rental Properties: Focus on properties that meet the needs of the local rental market and offer competitive amenities.

Property Flipping: Identify properties with renovation potential and opportunities to add value.

3. Financial Planning:

Rental Properties: Assess cash flow projections to ensure rental income covers expenses and generates positive cash flow.

Property Flipping: Create a detailed budget for renovations and factor in potential holding costs.

4. Risk Management:

Rental Properties: Plan for contingencies such as vacancies and maintenance costs.

Property Flipping: Anticipate potential renovation delays, unexpected costs, and market downturns.

5. Skill and Expertise:

Rental Properties: Property management skills are essential for tenant relations and property maintenance.

Property Flipping: Understanding property valuation, renovation processes, and market trends is crucial.

Both rental properties and property flipping can be lucrative real estate investment strategies, but they require different approaches and considerations. Rental properties provide passive income and long-term wealth accumulation, while property flipping offers the potential for short-term profits through active involvement in property transformation. Whether you choose one strategy or a combination of both, conducting thorough research, understanding market conditions, and assessing your financial capabilities will guide your investment decisions and help you achieve your real estate investment goals.

Navigating the World of Stocks and Investments

Investing in stocks and other investment vehicles is a dynamic journey that offers the potential for significant financial growth. While it comes with inherent risks, informed decision-making, a solid understanding of investment principles, and a well-defined strategy can help you navigate the complex world of investments and work towards your wealth-building goals. Here's a comprehensive guide to help you embark on your investment journey with confidence:

1. Understanding Stocks and Investments: Basics

- Stocks: Stocks represent ownership in a company. When you buy shares of a company's stock, you become a partial owner and have the potential to benefit from its growth and profitability.

- Investment Vehicles: Beyond stocks, there are various investment options, including bonds, mutual funds, exchange-traded funds (ETFs), real estate, commodities, and more. Each offers different risk and return profiles.

2. Set Clear Investment Goals: Defining Your Path

- Short-Term vs. Long-Term: Determine whether your investment goals are short-term (e.g., buying a house) or long-term (e.g., retirement).

- Risk Tolerance: Assess your comfort level with risk. Different investments come with varying levels of risk and potential return.

3. Develop a Diversified Portfolio: Spreading Risk

- Asset Allocation: Allocate your investments across different asset classes (stocks, bonds, real estate, etc.) to reduce risk. A diversified portfolio can help mitigate the impact of poor-performing investments.

4. Conduct Thorough Research: Informed Decisions

- Company Research: For stock investing, research companies' financial health, growth prospects, competitive advantages, and industry trends.

- Market Research: Stay informed about economic indicators, market trends, and geopolitical events that can impact your investments.

5. Risk Management: Mitigating Potential Losses

- Risk Assessment: Understand the risks associated with each investment. Higher potential returns often come with higher levels of risk.
- Portfolio Rebalancing: Regularly assess and adjust your portfolio to maintain your desired asset allocation.

6. Dollar-Cost Averaging: Consistent Investing

- Dollar-Cost Averaging: Invest a fixed amount of money at regular intervals (e.g., monthly) regardless of market conditions. This strategy reduces the impact of market volatility.

7. Understand Investment Vehicles: Choosing Wisely

- Stocks: Invest in companies with strong fundamentals, growth potential, and a competitive edge.
- Bonds: Consider bonds for income and capital preservation. Research their credit quality and interest rate risk.
- Mutual Funds and ETFs: These allow you to invest in diversified portfolios managed by professionals.

8. Seek Professional Guidance: Financial Advisors

- Financial Advisor: Consider working with a qualified financial advisor to create a customized investment strategy aligned with your goals and risk tolerance.

9. Patience and Discipline: Long-Term Outlook

- Long-Term Perspective: Investing is a journey. Focus on long-term growth rather than short-term market fluctuations.
- Discipline: Avoid emotional decisions driven by market volatility. Stick to your investment plan.

10. Continual Learning: Staying Informed

- Educate Yourself: Continuously learn about investment principles, economic trends, and financial markets.

11. Monitor and Adjust: Stay Proactive

- Regular Review: Periodically review your investment portfolio to ensure it remains aligned with your goals.

12. Start Early: The Power of Compounding

- Time Advantage: Starting early allows your investments more time to benefit from the power of compounding.

Navigating the world of stocks and investments requires a combination of research, informed decision-making, and a disciplined approach. By understanding your investment goals, assessing your risk tolerance, and crafting a diversified portfolio tailored to your needs, you can work towards building wealth over time. Remember that investing is a long-term endeavor, and while there may be ups and downs along the way, a well-thought-out strategy can help you achieve your financial aspirations and secure your future.

Stock Market Basics and Investment Strategies

The stock market is a dynamic arena where individuals can invest in companies and potentially reap financial rewards. Understanding the basics of the stock market and adopting effective investment strategies is essential for navigating this complex landscape and working towards your financial goals. Here's a comprehensive overview to help you get started:

1. **Stock Market Basics: Foundations**

Stocks (Equities): Stocks represent ownership in a company. When you buy shares of a company's stock, you become a shareholder, giving you the potential to benefit from the company's growth and profitability.

- Stock Exchanges: Stocks are bought and sold on stock exchanges such as the New York Stock Exchange (NYSE) and NASDAQ. These platforms facilitate the trading of stocks between buyers and sellers.

- Stock Price: The stock price reflects the value of a company's shares at any given moment. It can be influenced by factors like company performance, market sentiment, and economic conditions.

2. Investment Strategies: Approaches to Consider

1. Long-Term Investing:

- Buy and Hold: Invest in fundamentally strong companies with the intention of holding onto their stocks for an extended period, capitalizing on potential long-term growth.

- Value Investing: Seek undervalued stocks trading below their intrinsic value, with the expectation that their value will eventually be recognized by the market.

2. Growth Investing:

- Focus on Growth: Invest in companies with high potential for revenue and earnings growth, even if their current valuations seem high.
- Technology and Innovation: Look for industries that are at the forefront of technological advancements and innovation.

3. Dividend Investing:

- Dividend Stocks: Invest in companies that pay dividends to shareholders. Dividend payments can provide a consistent income stream.
- Dividend Growth: Focus on companies that not only pay dividends but also have a history of increasing dividend payouts over time.

4. Index Fund and ETF Investing:

- Passive Investing: Invest in index funds or exchange-traded funds (ETFs) that aim to replicate the performance of a specific market index.
- Diversification: Index funds and ETFs offer instant diversification across a broad range of stocks.

5. Sector Investing:

- Industry Focus: Invest in stocks within a specific sector or industry that you believe will experience significant growth.

3. Research and Due Diligence: Informed Decisions

- Company Analysis: Research a company's financial health, growth prospects, competitive advantages, and industry trends before investing.

- Market Analysis: Stay informed about economic indicators, market trends, and geopolitical events that can impact the stock market.

4. Risk Management: Mitigating Potential Losses

- Diversification: Spread your investments across different industries and sectors to reduce risk.
- Risk Tolerance: Assess your comfort level with risk and choose investments that align with your risk tolerance.

5. Consistent Contributions: Dollar-Cost Averaging

- Dollar-Cost Averaging: Invest a fixed amount of money at regular intervals (e.g., monthly) regardless of market conditions. This strategy reduces the impact of market volatility.

6. Professional Advice: Financial Advisors

- Financial Advisor: Consider working with a qualified financial advisor to create a personalized investment strategy based on your goals and risk tolerance.

7. Emotional Discipline: Stay the Course

- Avoid Emotional Decisions: Emotional reactions to market fluctuations can lead to impulsive decisions. Stick to your investment plan.

8. Continued Learning: Expanding Your Knowledge

- Educational Resources: Continuously educate yourself about investment principles, market trends, and financial news.

9. Monitor and Adjust: Stay Informed

- Regular Review: Periodically review your investment portfolio and adjust your strategy as needed based on changing circumstances.

10. Start Early: The Advantage of Time

- Compound Interest: Starting early allows your investments more time to benefit from the power of compounding.

Understanding the stock market basics and adopting effective investment strategies is crucial for building wealth over time. By setting clear investment goals, conducting thorough research, and adhering to a disciplined approach, you can navigate the complexities of the stock market with confidence. Remember that investing is a long-term endeavor, and a well-informed strategy will help you work towards achieving your financial aspirations and securing your future.

Diversifying Your Portfolio for Stability

Diversification is a fundamental principle of successful investing. It involves spreading your investments across a variety of assets to reduce risk and enhance the stability of your portfolio. By diversifying, you can potentially minimize the impact of poor-performing investments and capture the benefits of different asset classes. Here's how to effectively diversify your portfolio for greater stability:

1. Understand Diversification: The Importance

- Diversification involves investing in different types of assets, such as stocks, bonds, real estate, and more.

The goal is to create a mix of investments that are not highly correlated, meaning they don't all move in the same direction in response to market changes.

2. Asset Allocation: Building a Balanced Portfolio

- Stocks: Historically offer higher growth potential but come with higher risk.
- Bonds: Generally provide income and stability, acting as a buffer during market downturns.
- Real Estate: Offers potential for appreciation and rental income.
- Cash and Cash Equivalents: Provides liquidity and capital preservation.

3. Risk and Return: Balancing Act

- Risk Tolerance: Assess your comfort level with risk. Diversification can be tailored to your risk tolerance.
- Risk-Return Trade-Off: Higher-risk assets often have higher potential returns, but they also come with greater volatility.

4. Different Asset Classes: Broaden Your Reach

- Domestic and International: Diversify across different geographical regions to reduce country-specific risk.
- Equities and Fixed Income: Balance stocks and bonds based on your risk tolerance and investment goals.

5. Sector Diversification: Avoid Concentration

- Sectors: Invest in various sectors (e.g., technology, healthcare, finance) to avoid concentration risk in a single industry.
- Market Trends: Sector performance can vary based on economic conditions and trends.

6. Investment Styles: Blend Strategies

- Value and Growth: Invest in both value and growth stocks to capture opportunities across different market conditions.

7. Investment Vehicles: Variety Matters

- Individual Stocks and Bonds: Research companies and issuers before investing.

- Mutual Funds and ETFs: These funds provide instant diversification across a range of assets.

8. Rebalance Regularly: Maintain Alignment

- Review and Adjust: Periodically review your portfolio's allocation and rebalance to maintain your desired mix.

- Market Changes: Rebalancing allows you to capitalize on market movements.

9. Stay the Course: Long-Term Approach

- Patience: Diversification works best over the long term. Avoid making impulsive changes during market fluctuations.

10. Seek Professional Advice: Financial Advisors

- Expert Guidance: Consult a financial advisor to create a diversified portfolio tailored to your goals and risk tolerance.

11. Monitor and Adjust: Evolving Strategy

- Changing Goals: Adjust your portfolio as your financial goals and life circumstances change.

12. Continual Learning: Stay Informed

- Market Insights: Keep up with market trends, economic indicators, and geopolitical events.

Diversifying your portfolio is a prudent strategy for achieving stability and minimizing risk in your investments. By spreading your investments across various asset classes, sectors, and geographical regions, you can reduce the impact of market volatility on your overall portfolio performance. Remember that diversification doesn't eliminate risk entirely, but it can enhance the stability of your investments over the long term. Regularly reviewing and adjusting your portfolio as needed will help you stay on track to achieve your financial goals while managing risk effectively.

Entrepreneurial Ventures and Business Growth

Starting and growing an entrepreneurial venture requires a combination of creativity, strategy, perseverance, and adaptability. Whether you're launching a startup or seeking to expand an existing business, understanding key principles and strategies for entrepreneurship and business growth is essential. Here's a comprehensive guide to help you navigate the exciting journey of building and scaling your own business:

1. Entrepreneurial Mindset: Foundations of Success

- Passion and Vision: Identify a problem you're passionate about solving and envision how your business can make a positive impact.

- Resilience: Be prepared to face challenges and setbacks. An entrepreneurial journey is often marked by ups and downs.
- Innovation: Continuously seek new and creative ways to differentiate your business and offer unique value.

2. Market Research and Validation: Identifying Opportunities

- Target Audience: Define your ideal customers and understand their needs, preferences, and pain points.
- Market Analysis: Research your industry, competitors, and trends to identify gaps and opportunities.

- Product-Market Fit: Ensure that your product or service aligns perfectly with the needs of your target market.

3. Business Plan: Roadmap for Growth

- Mission and Strategy: Clearly define your business's mission, values, and long-term strategy.
- Financial Projections: Create realistic financial projections that outline revenue, expenses, and growth milestones.
- Action Steps: Develop a detailed plan of action for launching and growing your business.

4. Funding and Financing: Capitalizing Your Venture

- Bootstrapping: Fund your venture with personal savings and revenue generated by the business.

- Investors: Seek funding from angel investors, venture capitalists, or crowdfunding platforms.
- Loans and Grants: Explore options for business loans or grants offered by government agencies or organizations.

5. Building a Strong Team: People Power

- Talent Acquisition: Hire individuals who align with your business's values and have the skills needed to contribute to its growth.
- Delegation: Delegate tasks to team members to focus on strategic aspects of the business.
- Leadership: Lead by example, foster a positive company culture, and empower your team to succeed.

6. Marketing and Branding: Attracting Customers

- Brand Identity: Develop a compelling brand identity that resonates with your target audience.
- Online Presence: Establish a strong online presence through a professional website, social media, and content marketing.
- Customer Engagement: Build relationships with customers through personalized communication and exceptional service.

7. Scalability and Expansion: Growing Your Business

- Operational Efficiency: Streamline processes and operations to ensure smooth scalability.

- New Markets: Identify opportunities to expand into new geographic regions or target new customer segments.
- Product Line Extensions: Introduce complementary products or services to cater to evolving customer needs.

8. Innovation and Adaptation: Staying Relevant

- Continuous Improvement: Embrace a culture of continuous learning and improvement to adapt to changing market conditions.
- Innovative Solutions: Stay open to innovation and incorporate new technologies or business models as they emerge.

9. Customer Feedback and Iteration: Customer-Centric Approach

- Feedback Loop: Listen to customer feedback to make informed decisions and refine your offerings.
- Iterative Approach: Continuously iterate and enhance your products or services based on customer input.

10. Risk Management: Minimizing Challenges

- Contingency Planning: Develop contingency plans to address potential risks and challenges.
- Financial Resilience: Maintain a healthy financial position to weather unexpected downturns.

11. Legal and Regulatory Considerations: Compliance Matters

- Legal Structure: Choose the appropriate legal structure for your business, such as sole proprietorship, partnership, LLC, or corporation.
- Intellectual Property: Protect your intellectual property through patents, trademarks, copyrights, or trade secrets.
- Regulations: Understand and comply with industry-specific regulations and licensing requirements.

12. Exit Strategies: Planning for the Future

- Merger or Acquisition: Prepare for the possibility of being acquired by a larger company.

- Initial Public Offering (IPO): Explore the potential of taking your business public through an IPO.
- Succession Planning: Develop a succession plan to ensure a smooth transition if you decide to step away from the business.

Building and growing a successful entrepreneurial venture is a multifaceted journey that requires strategic thinking, adaptability, and a deep commitment to your vision. By embracing innovation, fostering a strong team, understanding your market, and adapting to changing circumstances, you can position your business for sustainable growth and long-term success. Remember that entrepreneurship is a dynamic and rewarding pursuit that offers the opportunity to make a lasting impact on the world while realizing your own aspirations.

From Idea to Business: Starting and Scaling Up

Turning your idea into a thriving business is an exhilarating and challenging endeavor. Whether you're just beginning or looking to scale up your existing venture, the process involves careful planning, strategic decision-making, and a strong dose of determination. Here's a comprehensive roadmap to guide you from the initial spark of an idea to the successful operation and growth of your business:

1. Idea Generation and Validation: Lay the Groundwork

- Identify a Problem: Recognize a problem or need that your product or service can address.

- Market Research: Conduct thorough research to understand your target audience, competitors, and market trends.
- Proof of Concept: Validate your idea by creating a prototype or minimum viable product (MVP) and gathering feedback from potential customers.

2. Business Planning: Create a Solid Foundation

- Business Model: Define your business model, including your value proposition, revenue streams, and customer segments.
- Mission and Vision: Establish a clear mission and vision for your business to guide your actions and decisions.
- Financial Projections: Develop realistic financial projections,

including revenue, expenses, and break-even points.

3. Legal and Structural Considerations: Get Legally Ready

- Legal Structure: Choose a legal structure that suits your business, such as sole proprietorship, partnership, LLC, or corporation.

- Permits and Licenses: Obtain any necessary permits, licenses, and registrations required to operate your business legally.

- Intellectual Property: Protect your intellectual property through patents, trademarks, copyrights, or trade secrets.

4. Funding and Financing: Secure Resources

- Bootstrapping: Fund your business with personal savings or revenue generated by the business.
- Investors: Seek funding from angel investors, venture capitalists, or crowdfunding platforms.
- Business Loans: Explore options for business loans from banks or financial institutions.

5. Product Development and Launch: Create and Introduce

- Product Refinement: Develop and refine your product or service based on feedback from your target audience.
- Marketing Strategy: Create a marketing plan to generate excitement

and anticipation for your product launch.

- Launch Plan: Strategically plan your launch, including marketing campaigns, sales channels, and distribution.

6. Customer Acquisition and Growth: Expand Your Reach

- Sales and Marketing: Implement strategies to attract and retain customers through advertising, social media, and other promotional tactics.

- Customer Relationship Management: Build strong relationships with customers through exceptional service and engagement.

7. Scaling Up: Take Your Business to the Next Level

- Operational Efficiency: Streamline processes and operations to accommodate increased demand.
- Team Building: Hire and train additional team members to support growth.
- Market Expansion: Explore new markets, products, or services to diversify your offerings.

8. Financial Management: Stay Profitable

- Cash Flow Management: Monitor and manage your cash flow to ensure you have enough resources to cover expenses and growth.
- Financial Analysis: Regularly review financial reports to track performance and make informed decisions.

9. Innovation and Adaptation: Embrace Change

- Continuous Improvement: Encourage a culture of innovation to stay relevant and adapt to changing market conditions.
- Feedback Loop: Gather feedback from customers to improve your products and services.

10. Leadership and Vision: Lead Your Team

- Inspire and Motivate: Lead by example and inspire your team to share your vision and commitment.
- Effective Communication: Maintain clear and open communication with your team to foster collaboration and alignment.

11. Risk Management: Mitigate Challenges

- Risk Assessment: Identify potential risks and develop strategies to mitigate them.
- Contingency Planning: Have backup plans in place to address unexpected setbacks.

12. Networking and Partnerships: Collaborate for Success

- Industry Connections: Build a network of mentors, advisors, and peers to share insights and experiences.
- Partnerships: Collaborate with complementary businesses or individuals to expand your reach.

13. Long-Term Sustainability: Plan for the Future

- Sustainability: Consider the long-term impact of your business on the environment and society.
- Succession Planning: Develop a plan for the continuity of your business in case of unforeseen events.

From idea to business, the path is filled with challenges, triumphs, and growth opportunities. By diligently following each step, adapting to changes, and staying focused on your mission, you can transform your entrepreneurial vision into a thriving reality. Remember that perseverance, innovation, and a customer-centric approach are the pillars that will guide you as you build and scale a successful business that makes a positive impact on your life and the world around you.

Financial Management in Entrepreneurship

Effective financial management is a critical component of entrepreneurship, ensuring that your business not only survives but thrives in a competitive landscape. Whether you're launching a startup or managing an established venture, understanding financial principles and adopting sound practices is essential for sustainable growth. Here's a comprehensive guide to help you navigate the realm of financial management in entrepreneurship:

1. Financial Planning: Building a Solid Foundation

- Budgeting: Create a detailed budget that outlines projected income and expenses.
- Cash Flow Forecasting: Estimate incoming and outgoing cash flows to ensure you have adequate liquidity.
- Financial Goals: Set clear financial objectives that align with your business's growth and sustainability.

2. Startup Costs and Funding: Getting off the Ground

- Startup Costs: Identify and calculate all expenses required to launch your business, including equipment, licenses, marketing, and more.
- Funding Sources: Explore various funding options such as personal savings, loans, grants, angel investors, and venture capital.

- Investor Pitch: Prepare a compelling pitch to attract potential investors by showcasing your business's potential for growth and profitability.

3. Accounting and Recordkeeping: Organizing Your Finances

- Accounting System: Choose an accounting software or hire an accountant to keep track of income, expenses, and financial transactions.
- Separate Business and Personal Finances: Maintain separate bank accounts and financial records for your business and personal expenses.
- Invoicing and Payment: Implement a consistent invoicing process to ensure timely payment from customers.

4. Financial Statements: Understanding Your Business's Health

- Income Statement: Also known as the profit and loss statement, it shows your revenues, expenses, and net income over a specific period.

- Balance Sheet: Provides a snapshot of your business's financial position by showing assets, liabilities, and owner's equity.

- Cash Flow Statement: Tracks cash inflows and outflows, helping you manage cash flow effectively.

5. Profitability and Cost Analysis: Maximizing Returns

- Gross Profit Margin: Calculate your gross profit by subtracting the cost of goods sold (COGS) from total revenue.

- Net Profit Margin: Determine your net profit by subtracting all expenses from total revenue.
- Break-Even Analysis: Identify the point at which your total revenue equals total costs, indicating the level of sales needed to cover expenses.

6. Managing Expenses: Efficiency and Control

- Cost Control: Monitor and manage expenses to avoid overspending and ensure profitability.
- Variable vs. Fixed Costs: Differentiate between costs that change with sales volume (variable) and those that remain constant (fixed).

7. Working Capital Management: Ensuring Liquidity

- Accounts Receivable: Monitor outstanding payments and follow up with customers to ensure timely collection.
- Accounts Payable: Manage vendor relationships to optimize payment terms and cash flow.

8. Investment and Capital Expenditures: Strategic Spending

- Capital Expenditures (CapEx): Allocate funds for investments in assets such as equipment, technology, and facilities.
- Return on Investment (ROI): Evaluate the potential return on capital expenditures to ensure they contribute to business growth.

9. Debt Management: Balancing Debt and Equity

- Debt Financing: Evaluate the benefits and risks of taking on debt to fund your business's operations or expansion.
- Debt Repayment: Develop a plan to repay loans on time to maintain a healthy credit history.

10. Financial Decision-Making: Informed Choices

- Data-Driven Decisions: Base financial decisions on accurate data and projections rather than assumptions.
- Scenario Analysis: Evaluate multiple scenarios to assess potential outcomes before making major financial choices.

11. Tax Planning: Minimizing Tax Liability

- Tax Strategy: Work with a tax professional to develop a tax-efficient strategy that minimizes your business's tax liability.
- Tax Deductions: Identify eligible tax deductions and credits that can reduce your tax burden.

12. Continuous Monitoring: Staying Informed

- Regular Review: Continuously monitor financial statements, cash flow, and key performance indicators to ensure your business remains on track.

Financial management is the backbone of successful entrepreneurship. By establishing sound financial practices, planning strategically, and making informed decisions, you can create a solid financial foundation for your business's growth and prosperity. Remember that financial management is an ongoing process that requires diligence, adaptability, and a commitment to the financial health of your business.

Tax Strategies for Wealth Optimization

Strategically managing your taxes is a crucial component of wealth optimization. By implementing effective tax strategies, you can legally minimize your tax liabilities, preserve more of your income and investments, and ultimately accelerate your path towards financial goals. Here's a comprehensive guide to help you navigate the world of tax optimization for wealth accumulation:

1. Understand Your Tax Landscape: The Basics

- Tax Brackets: Understand how tax rates apply to different income levels and plan to optimize your income within these brackets.

- Types of Taxes: Familiarize yourself with various taxes, including income tax, capital gains tax, estate tax, and more.

2. Tax-Efficient Investing: Maximizing Investment Returns

- Tax-Advantaged Accounts: Invest in tax-advantaged accounts such as IRAs, 401(k)s, and HSAs to enjoy tax benefits while saving for retirement or medical expenses.

- Asset Location: Allocate investments based on their tax treatment—hold tax-efficient investments in taxable accounts and tax-inefficient investments in tax-advantaged accounts.

3. Capital Gains and Losses: Timing Matters

- Capital Gains Tax: Understand how short-term and long-term capital gains are taxed differently. Holding investments for over a year can lead to lower tax rates.
- Tax Loss Harvesting: Offset capital gains by selling investments that have decreased in value, which can help reduce your overall tax liability.

4. Deductions and Credits: Leveraging Tax Benefits

- Itemized Deductions: Itemize deductions if they exceed the standard deduction to lower your taxable income.
- Tax Credits: Utilize tax credits such as the Child Tax Credit, Earned Income

Tax Credit, and education credits to directly reduce your tax bill.

5. Retirement Planning: Tax-Advantaged Growth

- Contributions: Contribute the maximum allowed to retirement accounts like IRAs and 401(k)s to benefit from tax-deferred growth.
- Roth Conversions: Consider converting traditional retirement account funds to Roth accounts for tax-free withdrawals in retirement.

6. Estate Planning: Passing on Wealth Efficiently

- Estate Tax Planning: Understand the estate tax threshold and explore strategies to minimize estate taxes, such as gifting and setting up trusts.

- Beneficiary Designations: Review and update beneficiary designations on retirement accounts and life insurance policies to ensure a smooth transfer of assets.

7. Business Tax Strategies: Entrepreneurial Considerations

- Entity Structure: Choose a business entity that aligns with your tax goals, such as sole proprietorship, LLC, S corporation, or C corporation.
- Deductible Expenses: Maximize business deductions by accurately tracking and documenting business-related expenses.

8. Charitable Giving: Giving Back While Benefitting

- Charitable Contributions: Donate to qualified charitable organizations to receive tax deductions for your contributions.
- Donor-Advised Funds: Consider setting up a donor-advised fund to make charitable contributions while optimizing your tax strategy.

9. Tax Planning Professionals: Expert Guidance

- Tax Advisors: Consult with tax professionals, such as certified public accountants (CPAs), tax attorneys, or financial advisors, to develop tailored tax strategies.

10. Stay Informed and Proactive: Ongoing Monitoring

- Tax Law Changes: Stay updated on changes in tax laws that could impact your tax strategies.
- Regular Review: Continuously review and adjust your tax strategies to align with your changing financial situation and goals.

Optimizing your taxes requires a proactive and well-informed approach. By leveraging legal tax strategies and making strategic financial decisions, you can keep more of your hard-earned money and channel it towards wealth accumulation, investments, and achieving your financial aspirations. Remember that tax optimization is an ongoing process, and staying informed about tax regulations and changes will help

you continue to make the most of your
financial opportunities.

Understanding Tax Efficiency and Minimization

Tax efficiency and minimization involve strategies and practices aimed at legally reducing your tax burden while optimizing your overall financial situation. By effectively managing your taxes, you can preserve more of your income, investments, and assets, allowing you to achieve your financial goals faster. Here's a comprehensive guide to help you gain a deeper understanding of tax efficiency and minimization:

1. Tax Efficiency vs. Tax Minimization: Key Differences

- Tax Efficiency: Focuses on structuring your financial affairs to minimize taxes while maximizing overall financial returns.

- Tax Minimization: Involves taking proactive steps to reduce your tax liability through legal strategies and deductions.

2. Taxable Income and Tax Liability: The Basics

- Taxable Income: The portion of your income that is subject to taxation after accounting for deductions, exemptions, and credits.

- Tax Liability: The amount of taxes you owe to the government based on your taxable income and the applicable tax rates.

3. Tax Efficiency Principles: Optimizing Your Strategy

- Timing: Strategically time income and expenses to lower your tax liability in a given year.

- Asset Location: Allocate investments among taxable and tax-advantaged accounts to minimize taxes on investment returns.

- Tax-Aware Investing: Consider the tax implications of investment decisions, such as holding investments with lower turnover and tax-efficient ETFs.

4. Tax-Advantaged Accounts: Maximizing Benefits

- Retirement Accounts: Contribute to 401(k)s, IRAs, or other retirement accounts to enjoy tax-deferred or tax-free growth.
- Health Savings Accounts (HSAs): Utilize HSAs to save for medical expenses with pre-tax dollars and tax-free withdrawals for qualified medical costs.

5. Tax Deductions and Credits: Leveraging Opportunities

- Standard Deduction vs. Itemized Deductions: Choose the option that results in greater tax savings.
- Tax Credits: Take advantage of tax credits to directly reduce your tax liability.

6. Capital Gains and Losses: Managing Investments Tax-Efficiently

- Long-Term vs. Short-Term Capital Gains: Long-term gains are typically taxed at lower rates than short-term gains.
- Tax Loss Harvesting: Offset capital gains with capital losses to minimize your overall tax liability.

7. Estate Planning: Passing on Wealth Strategically

- Estate Tax Considerations: Understand the estate tax threshold and explore strategies to minimize potential estate taxes.
- Gift Tax Exclusion: Take advantage of the annual gift tax exclusion to transfer wealth to heirs tax-free.

8. Tax-Efficient Spending: Budgeting and Expenses

- Tax-Efficient Withdrawal Strategy: Plan withdrawals from retirement accounts to minimize tax liability in retirement.
- Flexible Spending Accounts (FSAs): Utilize FSAs to pay for eligible medical and dependent care expenses with pre-tax dollars.

9. Business and Investment Strategies: Impact on Taxes

- Business Deductions: Maximize deductions for business-related expenses to reduce taxable income.
- Tax-Efficient Investments: Choose investments that generate tax-efficient returns, such as qualified dividends and tax-free bonds.

10. Professional Advice: Working with Tax Professionals

- Tax Advisors: Consult certified tax professionals, such as CPAs or tax attorneys, for personalized guidance on tax efficiency strategies.

11. Stay Informed and Adaptable: Changing Regulations

- Tax Law Changes: Stay updated on tax law changes that may impact your tax planning strategies.

- Adaptability: Adjust your strategies as your financial situation and tax laws evolve.

Understanding tax efficiency and minimization empowers you to make strategic financial decisions that align with your goals. By taking advantage of available tax-advantaged accounts, deductions, credits, and investment strategies, you can optimize your tax situation and retain more of your hard-earned money. Remember that tax planning is an ongoing process, and working with professionals and staying informed will help you navigate the complexities of the tax landscape while building a strong foundation for your financial future.

Legal Tax-Reduction Strategies for Investors and Business Owners

Investors and business owners have unique opportunities to implement legal tax-reduction strategies that can significantly lower their tax liabilities. These strategies can help you retain more of your earnings, invest in growth, and achieve your financial goals. Here's a comprehensive guide to legal tax-reduction strategies tailored for investors and business owners:

1. Tax-Advantaged Investment Accounts: Investors' Edge

- Individual Retirement Accounts (IRAs): Contribute to traditional IRAs for tax-deductible contributions or

Roth IRAs for tax-free withdrawals in retirement.

- 401(k) and Employer-Sponsored Plans: Contribute to employer-sponsored retirement plans to enjoy tax-deferred growth and potential employer matching.
- Health Savings Accounts (HSAs): Utilize HSAs for tax-free savings on medical expenses.

2. Capital Gains Tax Strategies: Investors' Advantage

- Long-Term Capital Gains: Hold investments for over a year to qualify for lower long-term capital gains tax rates.
- Tax Loss Harvesting: Offset capital gains with capital losses to minimize your tax liability.

3. Qualified Dividend Income: Lower Tax Rates

- Dividend Tax Rates: Qualified dividends may be taxed at lower rates than ordinary income.
- Dividend Stocks: Invest in companies that pay qualified dividends to benefit from reduced tax rates.

4. Real Estate Investors: Deductions and Benefits

- Depreciation Deduction: Real estate investors can deduct a portion of the property's cost over time, reducing taxable income.
- 1031 Exchange: Consider a like-kind exchange to defer capital gains tax when selling and reinvesting in another property.

- Passive Activity Loss Rules: Be aware of rules that limit deductions for passive real estate losses.

5. Small Business Owners: Deductions and Credits

- Business Expenses: Deduct ordinary and necessary business expenses, including rent, supplies, salaries, and marketing.
- Home Office Deduction: Claim a deduction if you have a dedicated space for conducting business at home.
- Qualified Business Income (QBI) Deduction: Benefit from a deduction of up to 20% of qualified business income for pass-through entities.

6. Startup Founders: Equity Compensation

- Stock Options and RSUs: Consider equity compensation to align your interests with the success of your company.
- Qualified Small Business Stock (QSBS): Potential exclusion of gain on qualified small business stock.

7. Tax Credits: Business Incentives

- Research and Development (R&D) Tax Credit: Claim credits for eligible R&D expenses.
- Work Opportunity Tax Credit (WOTC): Hire eligible employees to qualify for tax credits.

8. Estate Planning: Wealth Transfer Strategies

- Annual Gift Tax Exclusion: Gift assets up to a certain amount each year to reduce potential estate tax liability.
- Irrevocable Life Insurance Trust (ILIT): Transfer life insurance policies into an irrevocable trust for estate tax benefits.

9. Succession Planning: Smooth Transition

- Family Limited Partnership (FLP) or Limited Liability Company (LLC): Transfer assets to family members while retaining control.
- Buy-Sell Agreement: Plan for business succession by outlining the terms of ownership transfer.

10. Tax Planning Professionals: Expert Advice

- Tax Advisors: Consult with tax professionals to ensure you're utilizing the most advantageous strategies for your situation.

11. Stay Informed: Tax Law Updates

- Tax Law Changes: Stay updated on changes in tax laws that could impact your strategies.

Investors and business owners have a range of legal options to optimize their tax situations. By strategically leveraging tax-advantaged accounts, deductions, credits, and industry-specific strategies, you can reduce your tax liability while directing resources towards growth and wealth accumulation. It's important to work with tax professionals to tailor these strategies to your individual circumstances and goals. With careful planning and adherence to legal guidelines, you can navigate the complexities of taxation while building a strong financial foundation for yourself and your ventures.

Planning for Retirement and Long-Term Wealth

Retirement planning is a crucial endeavor that requires careful consideration, strategic decision-making, and disciplined savings. By developing a comprehensive retirement plan and focusing on long-term wealth accumulation, you can enjoy financial security and a comfortable lifestyle during your golden years. Here's a comprehensive guide to help you navigate the process of retirement planning and building lasting wealth:

1. Retirement Goals and Timeline: Setting the Stage

- Define Your Retirement Goals: Determine the lifestyle you envision for your retirement years, including travel, hobbies, and daily expenses.

- Estimate Your Retirement Timeline: Consider the age at which you plan to retire and calculate the number of years your retirement savings need to support you.

2. Financial Assessment: Knowing Where You Stand

- Evaluate Current Financial Position: Assess your assets, liabilities, income, and expenses to understand your financial situation.
- Project Future Expenses: Estimate future expenses in retirement, accounting for healthcare, housing, leisure, and other costs.

3. Retirement Savings Vehicles: Building a Nest Egg

- Employer-Sponsored Retirement Plans: Contribute to 401(k)s, 403(b)s, or similar plans to benefit from tax-deferred growth and potential employer matching.

- Individual Retirement Accounts (IRAs): Contribute to traditional IRAs or Roth IRAs based on your tax and retirement goals.

- Health Savings Accounts (HSAs): Maximize contributions to HSAs to cover medical expenses in retirement.

4. Compound Interest and Early Start: The Power of Time

- Start Early: The sooner you begin saving, the more time your investments have to grow through the power of compound interest.

- Regular Contributions: Consistently contribute to retirement accounts to harness the benefits of compounded returns.

5. Investment Strategy: Growing Your Wealth

- Diversification: Allocate investments across various asset classes to manage risk and enhance returns.
- Risk Tolerance: Align your investment choices with your risk tolerance and timeline.

6. Social Security and Pension: Government Benefits

- Social Security: Understand how Social Security benefits work and decide when to start claiming them based on your needs.

- Pension Plans: If applicable, review your pension options and consider how they fit into your overall retirement income strategy.

7. Retirement Income Needs: Creating a Sustainable Plan

- Withdrawal Strategy: Develop a sustainable withdrawal plan to ensure your savings last throughout retirement.
- Safe Withdrawal Rate: Consider the 4% rule or other safe withdrawal strategies to avoid outliving your savings.

8. Long-Term Care Planning: Addressing Healthcare Costs

- Long-Term Care Insurance: Evaluate whether long-term care insurance is necessary to cover potential healthcare expenses.
- Medicare and Medicaid: Understand the benefits and coverage provided by these government programs.

9. Estate Planning: Passing on Your Legacy

- Wills and Trusts: Create a will to outline your wishes for asset distribution and consider setting up trusts for more complex estate planning.
- Beneficiary Designations: Review and update beneficiary designations on retirement accounts and life insurance policies.

10. Regular Review and Adjustments: Adapting to Change

- Ongoing Assessment: Continuously monitor your retirement plan and make adjustments as your circumstances evolve.
- Inflation: Account for the impact of inflation on your retirement expenses and adjust your savings goals accordingly.

11. Professional Advice: Expert Guidance

- Financial Advisors: Consult with financial advisors specializing in retirement planning to create a tailored strategy.

12. Stay Informed: Evolving Retirement Landscape

- Retirement Trends: Stay updated on changes in retirement trends, regulations, and investment options.

Retirement planning is a journey that requires careful planning, disciplined savings, and informed decision-making. By setting clear goals, implementing a robust savings strategy, and staying attuned to your financial situation, you can enjoy a secure and fulfilling retirement. Remember that proactive planning, diversification, and regular adjustments are key to navigating the evolving financial landscape and ensuring a comfortable and prosperous retirement journey.

Retirement Accounts and Investment Planning

Retirement accounts and investment planning play a pivotal role in ensuring a financially secure retirement. By strategically utilizing retirement accounts and making informed investment decisions, you can build a strong financial foundation that supports your retirement goals. Here's a comprehensive guide to help you understand retirement accounts, investment strategies, and how they work together to create a prosperous retirement:

1. Types of Retirement Accounts: Tailoring Your Approach

- 401(k) and 403(b) Plans: Employer-sponsored plans that allow contributions from your paycheck, often with employer matching.

- Traditional IRA: Allows tax-deductible contributions, with taxes paid upon withdrawal in retirement.
- Roth IRA: Contributions are made with after-tax income, and qualified withdrawals in retirement are tax-free.
- SEP IRA and SIMPLE IRA: Retirement plans for self-employed individuals or small businesses.

2. Benefits of Retirement Accounts: Tax Advantages

- Tax-Deferred Growth: Investments within retirement accounts grow tax-deferred until withdrawal.
- Tax-Free Growth (Roth): Contributions are made after tax, but qualified withdrawals are tax-free.

- Reduced Tax Liability: Contributions to traditional retirement accounts may be tax-deductible.

3. Investment Strategies for Retirement Accounts: Maximizing Returns

- Diversification: Spread investments across asset classes to manage risk.
- Asset Allocation: Determine the right mix of stocks, bonds, and other investments based on your risk tolerance and timeline.
- Age-Based Strategies: Adjust your asset allocation as you approach retirement to reduce risk exposure.

4. Dollar-Cost Averaging: Consistency in Investment

- Dollar-Cost Averaging: Invest a fixed amount of money at regular intervals, reducing the impact of market volatility.

5. Employer Matching: Capitalizing on Contributions

- Employer Matching: Contribute enough to your employer-sponsored plan to receive the maximum matching contribution.

6. Investment Options: Choices Within Retirement Accounts

- Mutual Funds and ETFs: Diversified investment options that offer exposure to various markets.
- Target-Date Funds: Automatically adjust your asset allocation based on your retirement date.
- Individual Stock and Bonds: Build a customized portfolio based on your investment preferences.

7. Rebalancing: Maintaining Your Asset Allocation

- Regular Rebalancing: Adjust your portfolio periodically to ensure it aligns with your target asset allocation.

8. Risk Tolerance and Timeline: Balancing Risk and Return

- Risk Tolerance: Determine your comfort level with market fluctuations and select investments accordingly.
- Investment Timeline: Consider your investment horizon and adjust your strategy as you get closer to retirement.

9. Investment Monitoring: Staying Informed

- Regular Review: Periodically assess your portfolio's performance and make adjustments as needed.

10. Professional Advice: Expert Guidance

- Financial Advisors: Seek advice from financial professionals who specialize in retirement and investment planning.

11. Stay Informed: Evolving Investment Landscape

- Market Trends: Stay updated on market trends, economic conditions, and investment opportunities.

Retirement accounts and investment planning are fundamental to your retirement success. By selecting the right retirement accounts, strategically allocating your investments, and maintaining a balanced approach, you can work towards achieving your retirement goals. Remember that investment planning is a continuous process that requires ongoing monitoring, adjustments, and a willingness to adapt to changing market conditions. With a well-informed and disciplined approach, you can create a solid financial foundation that supports a comfortable and fulfilling retirement journey.

Creating a Sustainable Income Stream for Retirement

Creating a sustainable income stream for retirement is essential to maintain your desired lifestyle and financial security during your golden years. By implementing thoughtful strategies and optimizing your retirement assets, you can generate a consistent and reliable income that supports your needs and aspirations. Here's a comprehensive guide to help you navigate the process of building a sustainable retirement income:

1. Assess Your Retirement Needs: Setting the Foundation

- Estimate Expenses: Calculate your expected retirement expenses, including housing, healthcare, leisure, and daily living costs.

- Consider Inflation: Account for the impact of inflation on your future expenses.

2. Retirement Savings: Your Financial Toolkit

- Employer-Sponsored Plans: Utilize 401(k)s, 403(b)s, or similar plans to accumulate retirement savings over your career.

- Individual Retirement Accounts (IRAs): Contribute to traditional IRAs or Roth IRAs based on your tax and retirement goals.

- Pension Plans and Social Security: Understand the benefits you'll receive from pension plans and Social Security.

3. Retirement Income Sources: Building a Diverse Portfolio

- Social Security Benefits: Plan when to claim Social Security to maximize your lifetime benefits.
- Pension Income: If applicable, understand your pension options and choose the one that aligns with your goals.
- Investment Income: Generate income from your investment portfolio, including dividend-paying stocks and bonds.
- Annuities: Consider annuities to provide a guaranteed stream of income in retirement.

4. Safe Withdrawal Rate: Preserving Your Principal

- The 4% Rule: Withdraw around 4% of your retirement savings annually to help ensure your funds last.
- Flexible Withdrawal Strategy: Adjust your withdrawals based on market conditions and your portfolio's performance.

5. Dividend Stocks and Bonds: Income-Generating Investments

- Dividend-Paying Stocks: Invest in companies that consistently pay dividends to provide ongoing income.
- Bonds: Include bonds in your portfolio to generate steady interest payments.

6. Annuities: Guaranteed Income

- Immediate Annuities: Exchange a lump sum for a guaranteed stream of income for life.
- Deferred Annuities: Accumulate funds over time and convert them into guaranteed income later.

7. Rental Properties: Real Estate Income

- Real Estate Investments: Consider rental properties to generate rental income in retirement.
- Property Management: Decide whether to manage properties yourself or hire a property management company.

8. Part-Time Work or Consulting: Stay Active

- Semi-Retirement: Explore part-time work, consulting, or freelancing to supplement your retirement income.

9. Tax-Efficient Withdrawals: Maximizing Income

- Withdrawal Sequence: Strategically withdraw from different retirement accounts to minimize tax implications.

- Roth Conversions: Consider converting traditional retirement accounts to Roth accounts for tax-free withdrawals.

10. Longevity Considerations: Planning for the Long Haul

- Life Expectancy: Estimate your life expectancy to ensure your income plan covers your needs.

11. Professional Advice: Expert Guidance

- Financial Advisors: Consult with financial advisors to create a personalized retirement income strategy.

12. Regular Review: Adapting to Change

- Ongoing Assessment: Continuously monitor your retirement income plan and make adjustments as needed.

Creating a sustainable income stream for retirement requires careful planning, diversification, and a focus on maximizing your resources. By combining various income sources, including Social Security, pensions, investments, and potentially part-time work, you can create a well-rounded income strategy that supports your financial needs and aspirations throughout your retirement years. Remember that a balanced approach, ongoing monitoring, and the expertise of financial professionals will help you build and maintain a secure and fulfilling retirement income stream.

Building and Preserving Wealth Across Generations

Building and preserving wealth across generations involves strategic planning and responsible management to ensure that your financial legacy continues to benefit your family and future generations. By implementing effective strategies, you can pass down financial knowledge, assets, and values that contribute to a lasting legacy of prosperity. Here's a comprehensive guide to help you navigate the process of building and preserving wealth across generations:

1. Education and Communication: Passing Down Financial Knowledge

- Financial Literacy: Educate family members about budgeting, investing, taxes, and other financial topics.
- Open Communication: Foster transparent discussions about money management, values, and long-term goals.

2. Estate Planning: Structuring Your Legacy

- Wills and Trusts: Create an estate plan that outlines your wishes for asset distribution and minimizes potential estate taxes.
- Revocable Living Trust: Transfer assets to a trust for smoother probate and asset management.

3. Gifting Strategies: Transferring Wealth

- Annual Gift Tax Exclusion: Make tax-free gifts to family members up to a certain amount each year.
- Lifetime Gift Exemption: Utilize the lifetime gift tax exemption to transfer larger amounts while minimizing taxes.
- Generation-Skipping Transfer Tax: Navigate tax-efficient strategies when transferring wealth to grandchildren.

4. Family Limited Partnerships (FLPs) and Limited Liability Companies (LLCs): Managing Assets

- Entity Structures: Establish FLPs or LLCs to hold and manage family assets, allowing for shared ownership and management.

Control and Governance: Define roles and responsibilities within the family entity to ensure effective decision-making.

5. Philanthropy and Charitable Giving: Leaving a Positive Impact

- Donor-Advised Funds: Set up a donor-advised fund to make charitable contributions while involving family members.
- Charitable Foundations: Establish a family foundation to support causes aligned with your family's values.

6. Education Funds and Trusts: Investing in Future Generations

- 529 Plans: Contribute to education savings accounts that offer tax benefits for funding future education expenses.
- Crummey Trusts: Create trusts that provide beneficiaries with access to

funds while utilizing the annual gift tax exclusion.

7. Long-Term Investment Strategies: Growing Family Wealth

- Diversification: Build diversified investment portfolios to manage risk and maximize returns.

- Multigenerational Investment Advisors: Work with financial professionals who specialize in multigenerational wealth management.

8. Continuity Planning: Ensuring Smooth Transitions

- Succession Planning: Plan for the smooth transfer of family assets and leadership roles to the next generation.

- Regular Reviews: Continuously assess your estate plan and adjust as family dynamics and financial goals evolve.

9. Tax-Efficient Wealth Transfer: Minimizing Tax Implications

- Step-Up in Basis: Understand how inherited assets receive a stepped-up basis, potentially reducing capital gains taxes.
- Estate Tax Considerations: Consider strategies to minimize potential estate tax liabilities, such as irrevocable life insurance trusts (ILITs).

10. Professional Advisors: Expert Guidance

- Estate Attorneys: Consult with legal professionals specializing in estate planning to ensure your strategies are legally sound.

- Financial Advisors: Work with financial advisors experienced in multigenerational wealth management to develop a comprehensive plan.

11. Regular Family Meetings: Collaboration and Unity

- Family Council: Organize regular meetings to discuss financial matters, investmentb strategies, and charitable initiatives.

12. Values-Based Approach: Nurturing a Legacy

- Shared Values: Pass down family values alongside financial assets to preserve a sense of purpose and unity.

Building and preserving wealth across generations requires careful planning, open communication, and a commitment to passing down not only financial assets but also values and knowledge. By implementing strategies that align with your family's goals and values, you can create a legacy of financial success that positively impacts future generations. Remember that building and preserving wealth is an ongoing process that requires adaptation, collaboration, and the guidance of experienced professionals to ensure a prosperous financial future for your family.

Overcoming Challenges on the Path to Wealth

The journey to wealth is often marked by challenges that can test your determination, resilience, and financial acumen. By recognizing and addressing these obstacles, you can better prepare yourself to overcome them and continue progressing toward your financial goals. Here's a comprehensive guide to help you navigate and conquer challenges on the path to wealth:

1. Debt Management: Tackling Financial Liabilities

- High-Interest Debt: Prioritize paying off high-interest debt like credit card balances to prevent interest from accumulating.

- Debt Consolidation: Consider consolidating debts into a single loan with a lower interest rate.

2. Limited Income and Expenses: Maximizing Resources

- Budgeting: Create a detailed budget to track your income and expenses and identify areas for potential savings.
- Increase Income: Explore opportunities to increase your income through side gigs, freelancing, or career advancement.

3. Lack of Financial Education: Gaining Knowledge

- Self-Education: Invest time in learning about personal finance, investing, and wealth-building strategies.

- Financial Advisors: Seek advice from financial professionals to gain insights tailored to your situation.

4. Market Volatility: Navigating Investment Challenges

- Diversification: Spread investments across different asset classes to minimize risk from market fluctuations.
- Long-Term Perspective: Focus on long-term goals and avoid making impulsive decisions based on short-term market trends.

5. Unforeseen Emergencies: Building Financial Resilience

- Emergency Fund: Establish an emergency fund to cover unexpected expenses and avoid going into debt.

- Insurance Coverage: Ensure you have adequate insurance coverage for health, property, and other potential risks.

6. Lifestyle Inflation: Managing Expenses as Income Increases

- Savings Discipline: Maintain a consistent savings rate even as your income grows to avoid unnecessary spending.
- Delayed Gratification: Prioritize long-term financial goals over short-term indulgences.

7. Procrastination: Taking Action Promptly

- Start Early: Begin saving and investing as soon as possible to benefit from the power of compound interest.

- Automate Savings: Set up automatic transfers to savings and investment accounts to ensure consistency.

8. Impulse Spending: Practicing Financial Discipline

- Budgeting: Create a budget that allocates funds for both essential expenses and discretionary spending.
- Mindful Purchases: Pause before making impulse purchases and consider whether they align with your financial goals.

9. Changing Life Circumstances: Adapting to Challenges

- Life Transitions: Be prepared to adjust your financial plan in response to major life events like marriage, parenthood, or career changes.

- Flexible Planning: Build a financial plan that can accommodate unexpected shifts in circumstances.

10. Psychological Biases: Overcoming Behavioral Challenges

- Confirmation Bias: Seek out diverse perspectives when making financial decisions to avoid confirmation bias.
- Loss Aversion: Focus on the potential gains and long-term benefits of financial decisions.

11. Family and Social Pressures: Staying True to Your Goals

- Boundaries: Communicate your financial goals to loved ones and set boundaries around financial requests.
- Peer Pressure: Make financial decisions based on your values and goals, not external pressures.

12. Patience and Perseverance: Embracing the Journey

- Mindset: Cultivate patience and perseverance, recognizing that building wealth is a gradual process.

The path to wealth is not without challenges, but with the right strategies and mindset, you can overcome obstacles and continue progressing toward your financial goals. By addressing debt, managing expenses, staying informed, and practicing discipline, you can navigate challenges while building a strong financial foundation for your future. Remember that resilience, adaptability, and a commitment to your goals will empower you to overcome challenges and achieve lasting financial success.

Dealing with Setbacks and Financial Hardships

Financial setbacks and hardships are a natural part of life, but they don't have to define your financial journey. By approaching these challenges with resilience, adaptability, and strategic thinking, you can navigate difficult times and emerge stronger on the other side. Here's a comprehensive guide to help you effectively deal with setbacks and financial hardships:

1. Assess the Situation: Understanding the Scope

- Face Reality: Acknowledge the setback and assess its impact on your finances.

- Gather Information: Gather all relevant financial documents to understand your current situation.

2. Stay Calm and Emotionally Resilient: Managing Stress

- Emotional Well-Being: Prioritize your mental and emotional health to make clear-headed decisions.
- Positive Mindset: Maintain a positive outlook and focus on solutions rather than dwelling on the problem.

3. Create a Revised Budget: Adjusting Your Financial Plan

- Trim Expenses: Identify areas where you can cut discretionary spending temporarily to free up funds.
- Prioritize Essentials: Allocate your resources to cover necessary expenses like housing, utilities, and groceries.

4. Communicate and Seek Support: Reach Out for Help

- Talk Openly: Communicate your situation to family members, friends, and creditors if necessary.
- Financial Professionals: Consult financial advisors or credit counselors to get expert advice on managing your situation.

5. Explore Additional Income Streams: Supplementing Your Resources

- Side Gigs: Consider taking on temporary jobs, freelancing, or gig work to boost your income.
- Monetize Skills: Leverage your skills and hobbies to generate extra income.

6. Emergency Fund: Utilizing Your Safety Net

- Emergency Savings: Tap into your emergency fund to cover essential expenses during tough times.

7. Negotiate with Creditors: Managing Debt Obligations

- Contact Creditors: Reach out to lenders, landlords, and creditors to discuss possible payment adjustments.
- Interest Rates: Negotiate lower interest rates or payment plans to make debt more manageable.

8. Prioritize High-Interest Debt: Focusing on Financial Health

- Debt Repayment: Prioritize paying off high-interest debt to reduce financial strain.

9. Government Assistance and Resources: Exploring Options

- Unemployment Benefits: Apply for unemployment benefits if you've lost your job.
- Social Programs: Research government assistance programs that can offer temporary relief.

10. Evaluate Assets: Leveraging What You Have

- Sell Unused Items: Consider selling items you no longer need to generate extra cash.
- Liquidate Investments: If necessary, consider selling non-essential investments.

11. Focus on Long-Term Goals: Maintaining Perspective

- Stay Committed: Remember your long-term financial goals and stay focused on achieving them.

12. Learn and Adapt: Building Resilience

- Lessons Learned: Use setbacks as opportunities to learn about your financial strengths and weaknesses.
- Adaptability: Embrace change and adapt your financial strategies as needed.

Financial setbacks and hardships are challenges that can be overcome with the right approach. By remaining adaptable, seeking support, and taking practical steps to manage your finances, you can weather difficult times and position yourself for future success. Remember that setbacks are temporary, and by staying resilient and maintaining a proactive attitude, you can emerge from hardship even stronger than before.

Maintaining Resilience and Focus

Maintaining resilience and focus is key to successfully navigating life's challenges and pursuing your long-term goals. By developing a strong mindset, staying adaptable, and keeping your eyes on the bigger picture, you can overcome obstacles and achieve lasting success. Here's a comprehensive guide to help you cultivate resilience and stay focused:

1. Cultivating Resilience: Building Mental Strength
   - Positive Self-Talk: Replace negative thoughts with positive affirmations to maintain a resilient mindset.

- Embrace Failure: View setbacks as opportunities to learn and grow rather than as signs of defeat.

2. Practice Mindfulness: Staying Present and Grounded

- Mindful Awareness: Practice mindfulness techniques to stay present and reduce stress.
- Stress Management: Incorporate relaxation techniques like deep breathing and meditation into your routine.

3. Set Clear Goals: Anchoring Your Focus

- Specific Goals: Define clear and achievable short-term and long-term goals.
- Visualize Success: Imagine yourself achieving your goals to boost motivation and focus.

4. Prioritize Tasks: Effective Time Management

- To-Do Lists: Create organized lists to prioritize tasks and stay productive.
- Time Blocking: Allocate specific time blocks for focused work, minimizing distractions.

5. Adapt to Change: Embracing Flexibility

- Open-Mindedness: Embrace change as an opportunity for growth and new possibilities.
- Problem-Solving: Approach challenges with a solution-oriented mindset.

6. Surround Yourself with Positivity: Influencing Your Environment

- Supportive Network: Spend time with people who uplift and encourage you.

- Limit Negativity: Minimize exposure to negative news and influences.

7. Learn Continuously: Expanding Your Knowledge

- Continuous Learning: Stay curious and seek opportunities to learn and acquire new skills.
- Growth Mindset: Embrace challenges as opportunities to expand your capabilities.

8. Practice Self-Care: Nurturing Your Well-Being

- Physical Health: Prioritize exercise, nutrition, and adequate sleep for overall well-being.
- Hobbies and Interests: Engage in activities you enjoy to recharge and reduce stress.

9. Celebrate Progress: Acknowledging Achievements

- Small Wins: Recognize and celebrate even small steps toward your goals.

10. Stay Focused on Solutions: Moving Forward

- Solution-Focused Thinking: Shift your focus from problems to actionable solutions.
- Resist Overthinking: Avoid dwelling on negative thoughts and potential obstacles.

11. Seek Support: Reaching Out for Help

- Mentors and Advisors: Consult mentors or advisors for guidance and perspective.
- Professional Help: If needed, seek professional counseling to address mental and emotional challenges.

12. Embrace Challenges as Growth Opportunities: Rising Stronger

- Resilience as Growth: View challenges as opportunities to develop resilience and personal growth.

Maintaining resilience and focus is essential for overcoming life's challenges and achieving your aspirations. By cultivating a positive mindset, staying adaptable, and prioritizing self-care, you can navigate obstacles with strength and determination. Remember that resilience is a skill that can be developed and refined over time, leading you toward a future filled with accomplishments, growth, and a deep sense of purpose.

The Future of Wealth: Trends and Opportunities

As the world evolves, so does the landscape of wealth creation and management. Understanding emerging trends and embracing new opportunities is crucial for staying ahead in the realm of wealth building. Here's an insightful guide to help you anticipate the future of wealth, identify trends, and capitalize on emerging opportunities:

1. Technology and Digitalization: Revolutionizing Wealth Management
   - Fintech Innovations: Embrace advancements in financial technology, from robo-advisors to digital wallets, for efficient wealth management.

- Cryptocurrencies and Blockchain: Explore the potential of cryptocurrencies and blockchain technology for diversifying investment portfolios.

2. Sustainable Investing: Integrating Environmental and Social Impact

- ESG Investments: Engage in environmentally and socially responsible investing to align your wealth growth with positive impact.
- Impact Investing: Seize opportunities to invest in projects that generate social and environmental benefits alongside financial returns.

3. Remote Work and Entrepreneurship: Redefining Income Streams

- Remote Income Streams: Capitalize on the flexibility of remote work and online platforms to diversify income sources.
- Online Businesses: Leverage e-commerce, freelancing, and digital entrepreneurship for creating new avenues of wealth generation.

4. Artificial Intelligence and Automation: Transforming Financial Strategies

- AI-Driven Insights: Utilize AI for data analysis, predictive modeling, and personalized financial advice.
- Automated Investing: Implement algorithm-based investment strategies to optimize portfolio management.

5. Aging Population and Retirement: Rethinking Long-Term Financial Planning

- Silver Economy: Recognize the opportunities presented by an aging population for businesses and investments targeting seniors.
- Longevity Planning: Address the financial implications of increased life expectancy through comprehensive retirement planning.

6. Healthcare Innovation: Balancing Health and Wealth

- Health Tech: Invest in healthcare technologies that improve well-being and longevity.
- Healthcare Costs: Plan for rising healthcare expenses by exploring insurance options and health savings strategies.

7. Globalization and Emerging Markets: Expanding Investment Horizons

- Global Investments: Diversify your portfolio with exposure to emerging markets and international assets.
- International Real Estate: Consider real estate investments in growing global markets for potential appreciation.

8. Resilience and Crisis Preparedness: Safeguarding Wealth

- Emergency Funds: Maintain robust emergency funds to weather unexpected financial challenges.
- Risk Management: Prioritize insurance coverage to protect your assets and investments.

9. Education and Lifelong Learning: Fueling Personal and Financial Growth

- Continuous Learning: Invest in education and skill development to adapt to evolving industries and opportunities.
- Future-Proofing Skills: Stay ahead by acquiring skills relevant to emerging sectors such as AI, renewable energy, and sustainable technologies.

10. Intergenerational Wealth Transfer: Legacy and Succession Planning

- Family Governance: Implement structures and strategies to ensure smooth wealth transfer across generations.

- Education for Heirs: Educate heirs about responsible wealth management and values-based financial decisions.

11. Environmental Awareness: Green Investing and Sustainable Practices

- Green Investments: Consider renewable energy, sustainable agriculture, and clean technology investments.
- Climate Change Risks: Assess investment risks related to climate change and seek opportunities for sustainable growth.

12. Cultural Shifts and Values-Based Investing: Aligning Wealth with Beliefs

- Values-Driven Choices: Invest in companies and projects that align with your personal values and beliefs.

The future of wealth is dynamic and full of opportunities. By staying informed about technological advancements, societal shifts, and global trends, you can position yourself to seize new avenues for growth and prosperity. Adapting your financial strategies to these evolving landscapes will empower you to create lasting wealth that aligns with your goals, values, and the changing world around you.

Emerging Technologies and Investment Trends

The ever-evolving technological landscape is shaping the way we invest and manage wealth. As new technologies emerge, they create exciting opportunities for investors to capitalize on innovative trends. Here's a comprehensive guide to help you navigate emerging technologies and investment trends that are shaping the future of finance:

1. Artificial Intelligence (AI) and Machine Learning: Smart Investing

- Algorithmic Trading: Utilize AI-driven algorithms to make data-informed investment decisions in real time.

- Robo-Advisors: Embrace automated investment platforms that tailor portfolios to your risk tolerance and goals.

2. Blockchain and Cryptocurrencies: Digital Assets and Beyond

- Cryptocurrencies: Explore the potential of digital currencies like Bitcoin and Ethereum as alternative investment assets.
- Blockchain Applications: Beyond cryptocurrencies, consider blockchain's potential for revolutionizing supply chains, contracts, and more.

3. Augmented Reality (AR) and Virtual Reality (VR): Transforming Industries

- Real Estate Investment: Utilize AR and VR for virtual property tours, enhancing real estate investment decision-making.
- Entertainment and Media: Invest in AR and VR content platforms that are shaping the future of entertainment.

4. 5G Technology: Connectivity and Communication

- Internet of Things (IoT): Invest in IoT technologies that leverage 5G connectivity for smart homes, cities, and industries.
- Telecommunications: Consider telecom companies at the forefront of 5G deployment.

5. Biotechnology and Healthcare Innovations: Health and Wealth

- Genomics: Invest in companies at the forefront of genetic research and personalized medicine.
- Telemedicine and Health Tech: Capitalize on the rise of virtual healthcare services and health-focused technology.

6. Renewable Energy and Sustainable Technologies: Green Investments

- Solar and Wind Energy: Explore opportunities in renewable energy production and storage.
- Battery Technology: Invest in companies driving advancements in energy storage solutions.

7. Electric and Autonomous Vehicles: Future of Transportation

- Electric Car Manufacturers: Consider companies leading the electric vehicle market.
- Autonomous Vehicle Technology: Invest in self-driving technology and related infrastructure.

8. Cybersecurity and Data Privacy: Protecting Digital Assets

- Cybersecurity Solutions: Invest in companies providing robust cybersecurity measures for individuals and businesses.
- Privacy Tech: Explore investments that protect user data and privacy in the digital age.

9. Space Exploration and Satellite Technology: Beyond Earth's Boundaries

- Space Tourism: Monitor developments in the emerging space tourism industry.
- Satellite Communication: Consider satellite technology companies enabling global connectivity.

10. Clean Water and Environmental Solutions: Addressing Global Challenges

- Water Technology: Invest in companies providing clean water solutions and water infrastructure.

11. E-Commerce and Digital Payments: Changing Consumer Behavior

- Online Retail: Capitalize on the growth of e-commerce platforms and online marketplaces.

- Digital Payments: Invest in fintech companies driving the transition to cashless transactions.

12. Quantum Computing: Computing Beyond Limits

- Quantum Computing: Monitor advancements in quantum computing with potential applications in various industries.

Emerging technologies are reshaping investment landscapes across diverse sectors. Staying informed about these trends and their potential impacts on industries will enable you to make strategic investment decisions that align with your financial goals and risk tolerance. By embracing these technological shifts, you position yourself to seize opportunities and shape a successful investment portfolio that reflects the future of finance.

Adapting to Evolving Economic Landscapes

In a rapidly changing world, adapting to evolving economic landscapes is essential for maintaining financial stability and achieving long-term success. By staying agile, informed, and proactive, you can navigate economic shifts and seize opportunities that arise. Here's a comprehensive guide to help you adapt effectively to changing economic conditions:

1. Continuous Learning: Knowledge as a Cornerstone

- Stay Informed: Keep up with economic news, trends, and policy changes that impact various sectors.

- Industry Insights: Gain a deep understanding of the industries you're invested in to make informed decisions.

2. Diversification: Spreading Risk

- Portfolio Diversification: Allocate investments across different asset classes to mitigate risks.
- Geographic Diversification: Consider international investments to reduce exposure to specific economic conditions.

3. Flexibility in Financial Planning: Adapting Strategies

- Review and Adjust: Regularly review your financial plan and adjust it to align with changing goals and economic circumstances.

- Emergency Fund: Maintain a robust emergency fund to weather economic downturns.

4. Scenario Planning: Preparing for Different Scenarios

- Best-Case and Worst-Case Scenarios: Develop plans for various economic scenarios to ensure you're prepared.
- Contingency Plans: Identify alternative strategies to navigate unexpected economic challenges.

5. Building Marketable Skills: Staying Employable

- Skill Development: Invest in skills that remain relevant in changing job markets.
- Adaptability: Be open to learning new skills as industries evolve.

6. Embracing Technology: Leveraging Digital Advancements

- Remote Work and Entrepreneurship: Utilize technology to explore remote work, freelancing, and online business opportunities.
- Digital Transformation: Invest in companies driving technological advancements and digital innovation.

7. Long-Term Investment Horizon: Patience and Planning

- Avoid Panic: Maintain a long-term perspective and avoid making impulsive decisions based on short-term fluctuations.
- Steady Contributions: Continue contributing to retirement accounts and investments regardless of short-term market trends.

8. Networking and Collaboration: Leverage Connections

- Professional Network: Cultivate relationships within your industry to stay informed about emerging opportunities.
- Collaboration: Partner with peers to navigate economic challenges through shared insights.

9. Addressing Debt: Managing Financial Obligations

- Debt Management: Prioritize paying down high-interest debt to reduce financial burden.
- Refinancing: Explore options to refinance loans during periods of low interest rates.

10. Entrepreneurial Mindset: Identifying Business Opportunities

- Identify Market Gaps: Look for opportunities to create or pivot businesses that cater to evolving consumer needs.
- Innovation: Innovate to address new challenges and meet changing demands.

11. Environmental Awareness: Sustainability and Resilience

- Sustainable Practices: Embrace environmentally conscious choices that contribute to long-term economic resilience.

12. Professional Advisors: Expert Guidance

- Financial Advisors: Consult professionals for advice on adapting your financial strategies to changing economic landscapes.

Adapting to evolving economic landscapes requires a combination of proactive planning, continuous learning, and the willingness to embrace change. By staying agile, informed, and prepared, you can not only navigate economic challenges but also position yourself to capitalize on emerging opportunities. Remember that resilience, flexibility, and a forward-looking approach will empower you to thrive amid economic transformations and achieve your financial goals.

Conclusion

The journey to financial success is a dynamic and transformative one, filled with challenges, opportunities, and moments of growth. Through the pages of this comprehensive guide, you've explored the intricacies of building wealth, navigating setbacks, embracing emerging trends, and adapting to evolving economic landscapes. As you conclude this journey, remember these key takeaways:

- Financial Mindset: Cultivate a wealth-building mindset that values discipline, perseverance, and a commitment to your long-term goals.

- Clear Goals: Set clear and achievable financial goals that guide your actions and priorities.
- Budgeting and Savings: Master the art of budgeting, saving consistently, and managing your money wisely.
- Investment Knowledge: Understand various investment vehicles, strategies, and the power of compounding to grow your wealth over time.
- Risk Management: Prioritize risk management through insurance, diversified portfolios, and informed decision-making.
- Entrepreneurial Spirit: Embrace entrepreneurial opportunities and innovative thinking for both career growth and income diversification.

- Tax Efficiency: Optimize your tax strategies to minimize liabilities and maximize wealth accumulation.
- Long-Term Planning: Plan for retirement, intergenerational wealth transfer, and a sustainable financial legacy.
- Resilience: Develop resilience to navigate setbacks, economic changes, and unexpected challenges.
- Adaptability: Stay informed about emerging technologies, trends, and economic shifts to make informed decisions.
- Lifelong Learning: Continue to learn, evolve, and acquire skills that align with changing industries and market demands.

- Positive Impact: Consider the social and environmental impact of your financial decisions, embracing values-based investing and sustainable practices.

Remember that building and preserving wealth is a continuous journey. Each step you take, each decision you make, contributes to your financial growth and the legacy you leave for generations to come. By staying committed, adaptable, and open to new opportunities, you can create a future of financial freedom and success. As you move forward, keep the lessons from this guide in mind and approach your financial journey with confidence and determination. Your path to lasting financial success begins today.

Reflecting on Your Wealth-Building Journey

As you pause to reflect on your wealth-building journey, take pride in the progress you've made and the lessons you've learned. This introspection allows you to acknowledge your achievements, refine your strategies, and set your sights on a future filled with even greater financial success. Here's a guide to help you reflect on your journey and chart your course for the road ahead:

1. Celebrate Milestones: Acknowledging Achievements

- Achievements: Recognize the milestones you've reached on your wealth-building journey.
- Progress: Reflect on the growth of your savings, investments, and financial knowledge.

2. Review Your Goals: Assessing Your Vision

- Initial Goals: Revisit the goals you set when you embarked on this journey.
- Achievements: Evaluate which goals you've achieved, adjusted, or expanded upon.

3. Lessons Learned: Wisdom from Experience

- Successes: Identify the strategies that have led to successful outcomes.

- Challenges: Reflect on the challenges you've faced and the lessons they've taught you.

4. Changes and Adaptations: Evolving Strategies

- Adaptation: Consider how you've adjusted your approach based on changing circumstances.
- New Opportunities: Reflect on the new opportunities you've seized along the way.

5. Financial Mindset: Cultivating Growth

- Mindset Shifts: Reflect on how your mindset has evolved in terms of money, wealth, and success.
- Resilience: Recognize your growing resilience in the face of setbacks.

6. Impact and Values: Aligning Wealth with Purpose

- Social Impact: Reflect on the ways your financial decisions have contributed to positive change.
- Values Alignment: Consider how your values influence your investment choices.

7. Future Vision: Setting New Horizons

- Long-Term Vision: Visualize where you want to be financially in the next 5, 10, or 20 years.
- New Goals: Set new goals that align with your evolving aspirations and priorities.

8. Continuous Learning: Fostering Growth

- Educational Path: Reflect on the new skills and financial knowledge you've acquired.
- Learning Curve: Acknowledge that learning is ongoing and embrace new opportunities to expand your knowledge.

9. Gratitude and Patience: Embracing the Journey

- Gratitude: Express gratitude for the progress you've made and the opportunities you've encountered.
- Patience: Recognize that building wealth is a gradual process that requires perseverance.

10. Your Legacy: Leaving a Lasting Impact

- Generational Impact: Reflect on how your financial decisions impact not only your life but also the lives of future generations.
- Legacy Building: Consider the ways you're shaping a financial legacy that reflects your values and aspirations.

11. Self-Care and Well-Being: Balancing Life and Wealth

- Balance: Reflect on how you've balanced your financial pursuits with personal well-being and relationships.
- Self-Care: Ensure that your financial journey supports your overall quality of life.

12. Next Steps: Moving Forward with Purpose

- Action Plan: Outline the specific steps you'll take to pursue your future financial goals.
- Commitment: Reaffirm your commitment to your financial journey and the principles that guide you.

Reflection is a powerful tool that empowers you to learn from the past, appreciate the present, and plan for the future. As you reflect on your wealth-building journey, recognize the progress you've made, the challenges you've overcome, and the wisdom you've gained. Use this reflection to chart a course that aligns with your aspirations, values, and vision for the future. Embrace the journey with enthusiasm, determination, and the knowledge that you have the tools to continue building a prosperous and fulfilling financial life.

Embracing a Life of Financial Freedom

Achieving financial freedom is more than a goal; it's a profound shift that empowers you to live life on your terms. As you embark on this transformative journey, you're making choices that lead to abundance, security, and the freedom to pursue your passions. Here's a guide to help you fully embrace a life of financial freedom:

1. Clarity of Purpose: Defining Your Vision

- Personal Vision: Envision the life you want to lead—free from financial constraints.

- Values Alignment: Ensure that your financial goals align with your core values and aspirations.

2. Strategic Planning: Your Blueprint to Freedom

- Financial Roadmap: Develop a comprehensive plan that outlines your short-term and long-term financial goals.
- Budget and Savings: Prioritize saving and smart spending to build a solid financial foundation.

3. Debt-Free Journey: Liberating Your Finances

- Debt Reduction: Strategically pay off debts to free up resources for wealth-building endeavors.

- Smart Borrowing: If necessary, make informed borrowing decisions that align with your financial goals.

4. Diversified Investments: Building Wealth

- Investment Portfolio: Create a diversified portfolio that aligns with your risk tolerance and financial goals.
- Compound Growth: Leverage the power of compounding to grow your investments over time.

5. Passive Income Streams: Liberating Your Time

- Multiple Streams: Establish passive income sources such as investments, real estate, or royalties.

- Time Freedom: Enjoy the flexibility to pursue your interests without being tied to a traditional 9-to-5 job.

6. Mindful Spending: Conscious Consumption

- Prioritize Value: Spend money on experiences and items that truly enrich your life.
- Avoid Lifestyle Inflation: Resist the urge to overspend as your income grows.

7. Resilience and Preparedness: Safeguarding Your Freedom

- Emergency Fund: Maintain a robust emergency fund to navigate unexpected financial challenges.

- Risk Management: Protect your investments and assets through insurance and careful planning.

8. Pursuing Passions: Living with Purpose

- Passion Projects: Allocate time and resources to pursuits that bring joy and fulfillment.
- Continued Learning: Embrace personal growth and skill development to enrich your life.

9. Legacy Building: Impact Across Generations

- Generational Wealth: Consider how your financial choices can positively impact your family's future.

- Philanthropy: Give back to causes that align with your values and create a lasting legacy.

10. Mindfulness and Well-Being: A Balanced Life

- Holistic Approach: Focus on well-being, health, and nurturing relationships in addition to financial success.
- Mindfulness Practices: Cultivate presence and gratitude to fully enjoy your journey.

11. Giving Back: Enriching the World

- Community Involvement: Engage in activities that contribute positively to your local community.

- Social Impact: Use your resources to support initiatives that create positive change.

12. Embracing the Journey: Living Free and Abundantly

- Mindset of Abundance: Embrace a mindset that acknowledges the abundance you've created in your life.
- Celebration: Celebrate milestones and achievements along the way.

Embracing a life of financial freedom is an empowering journey that grants you the autonomy to make choices aligned with your dreams and values. Through strategic planning, mindful decision-making, and a commitment to your vision, you're creating a life that is abundant, purposeful, and truly your own. As you navigate this path, remember that your journey of financial freedom is not just about wealth—it's about creating a life of meaning, impact, and joy.